Table Of Contents

Chapter 1: The Dawn Of AI In The Arts   7

    Introduction To AI Technologies   8

    Historical Perspective On Technology And Art   10

    Photography: Revolutionizing Visual Art in the 19th Century   16

    Mass Production: Shaping Popular Culture   19

    TV and Film: Revolutionizing Visual Storytelling   21

    Transforming the Artistic Landscape   24

    Early Examples Of AI In Creative Fields   29

Chapter 2: The Disruption Of Traditional Art Forms   38

    Case Studies Of AI Impacting The Arts   40

    Interviews with Artists and Creators on AI in Art   43

    Changes in Art Consumption and Production   45

Chapter 3: Enhancement Or End Of Creativity?   49

    Philosophical And Ethical Considerations Of AI In Art   51

    Perspectives From Critics And Art Historians   54

    The Debate Around Originality And Authenticity   56

Chapter 4: The AI Artist – Case Studies And Profiles   59

   Profiling AI Systems Known For Creative Outputs   60

   Interviews With Developers And Engineers   63

   Exploring The 'Artist' Identity Of AI   66

Chapter 5: Public And Critical Reception   69

   Analysis Of Public Reaction To AI-Generated Art   71

   How AI Art Has Been Received In Public   73

   Critical Reviews And Notable Critiques   76

Chapter 6: The Economic And Social Impact   79

   Effects On Job Markets   81

   Shifts In Art Education And Training   84

   Global Reach Of AI On Different Cultures   86

Chapter 7: The Future Of Creativity In The AI Era   90

   Predictions And Trends For AI In The Creative Sectors   92

   Future Technologies And Their Implications   95

   Dystopian And Utopian Visions   98

Chapter 8: Embracing AI – A New Paradigm For Creativity   101

   Shifting The Narrative From Competition To Collaboration   103

Successful Human-AI Creative Partnerships   105

Conclusion   109

Strategies For Artists And Creators To Adapt And Thrive   109

Conclusion   112

Chapter 9: Harnessing AI For Enhanced Creativity   113

Practical Tips For Integrating AI Into Artistic Processes   115

Conclusion   118

Tools And Platforms Facilitating AI-Assisted Creativity   118

Conclusion   121

Conclusion   123

Chapter 10: The Renaissance Of Creativity – AI As A Tool   125

Conclusion   127

Redefining The Role Of The Artist In The Age Of AI   127

Encouraging A Culture Of Experimentation   129

Case Studies Of Groundbreaking Works Created With AI   132

Conclusion   134

Chapter 11: The Future Symbiosis Of Human And AI   135

Vision For A Future   137

Conclusion   139

Ethical Guidelines For AI In The Arts   140

Conclusion   142

Final Thoughts...   143

Conclusion   145

Ideas for Using AI for Creativity: 146

In the heart of a rapidly evolving digital age, the advent of artificial intelligence (AI) has stirred a profound transformation in the world of art and creativity. "Artificial Muse" delves into this intricate and often controversial terrAIn, exploring the multifaceted relationship between AI and the creative arts. Our journey traverses the initial waves of disruption and the ensuing debates, leading to a visionary future where AI not only coexists with human creativity but enhances it.

This book is crafted to unravel the complexities of AI's role in the arts, examining its impact across various disciplines—music, literature, visual arts, and beyond. We start by retracing the steps of AI's emergence in creative fields, setting the stage for an in-depth analysis of how traditional art forms are being reshaped. Through case studies, interviews, and critical analysis, we capture the diverse voices of artists, technologists, critics, and consumers, pAInting a holistic picture of a world where art is no longer confined to human hands and minds.

Central to our narrative is a debate that has captivated philosophers, artists, and technologists alike: Does AI herald the end of creativity, or is it a new beginning? We delve into ethical considerations, originality, authenticity, and the evolving identity of the artist in the age of AI. This discourse is enriched by profiling AI systems known for creative outputs, exploring their 'artist' identity, and understanding the public and critical reception of AI-generated art.

As we navigate through the economic, social, and cultural impacts of AI in the arts, we arrive at a pivotal point. The book shifts from a discussion of AI as a disruptive force to a powerful ally in the creative process. We propose a new paradigm where artists and AI collaborate, leading to unprecedented forms of expression and innovation.

In the final chapters, "Artificial Muse" offers a treasure trove of practical insights and inspirational ideas for harnessing AI in creative endeavors. We present tools, platforms, and resources that enable artists to integrate AI into their work, not as a replacement, but as a partner in the creative process. This leads to a renAIssance of creativity, where AI is a tool, not a threat.

"Artificial Muse" is more than a book; it's a call to embrace a future where human and artificial creativity flourish in symbiosis. It is an invitation to artists, creators, and enthusiasts to explore, adapt, and thrive in this new landscape. Through this exploration, we AIm to inspire, inform, and ignite a conversation about the limitless possibilities that arise when we view AI not as the end of art, but as the beginning of a new chapter in creative expression.

Chapter 1: The Dawn Of AI In The Arts

As the first rays of dawn herald a new day, so too does the advent of artificial intelligence (AI) mark the beginning of a new era in the arts. This chapter, "The Dawn of AI in the Arts," is an exploration into the genesis of this transformative moment, tracing the initial threads of AI's integration into the creative world.

Our journey begins by delving into the origins of AI technology, demystifying its principles and mechanisms. We will explore the foundational milestones that have paved the way for AI's entry into the artistic arena, providing a backdrop to understand its current and potential impact. This exploration is not just technical but also historical, examining how past technological advancements have shaped and reshaped the arts.

We will then transition to real-world examples, showcasing early instances where AI has intersected with various art forms. From algorithmically generated music compositions to AI-authored prose and poetry, and from digital art installations to AI-driven theatre productions, these examples will illustrate the embryonic stages of AI's influence on creativity.

This chapter also introduces the voices of pioneering individuals who stand at the crossroads of AI and the arts. Artists, technologists, and innovators who have embraced AI in their creative processes share their insights and experiences. Their stories provide a unique perspective on the opportunities and challenges presented by this new tool in their artistic arsenal.

By examining the dawn of AI in the arts, we set the stage for a deeper understanding of this revolutionary intersection. This chapter is not just a historical account; it's a gateway into a world where art and technology converge, creating new languages, new forms, and new possibilities for expression. It invites readers to reflect on how AI, a creation of human ingenuity, is now partnering with its creators in the endless pursuit of beauty and meaning.

Introduction To AI Technologies

In the context of the arts, understanding the fundamentals of artificial intelligence (AI) is essential to appreciate its transformative impact. AI, at its core, refers to machines or systems capable of performing tasks that typically require human intelligence. These tasks include learning, reasoning, problem-solving, perception, and language understanding. The journey of AI in the arts is a confluence of these capabilities with creative processes, leading to a novel paradigm of artistic expression.

The Building Blocks of AI

Machine Learning (ML): Machine Learning is the backbone of modern AI. It involves training algorithms to learn patterns, make decisions, and predict outcomes based on data. In the arts, ML algorithms can analyze styles, genres, and techniques, learning to create new works that reflect learned patterns.

Neural Networks and Deep Learning: Inspired by the human brain's structure, neural networks are a series of algorithms that recognize underlying relationships in a set of data. Deep Learning, a subset of ML, involves neural networks with many layers (hence 'deep') that can learn from vast amounts of data. This technology drives the most advanced AI applications in image recognition, natural language processing, and even style transfer in art.

Natural Language Processing (NLP): NLP enables AI to understand, interpret, and respond to human language. In literary arts, NLP is used for tasks like generating poetry or prose, or for analyzing literary styles and themes.

Computer Vision: This involves enabling machines to interpret and understand visual information from the world, typically through digital images. In the realm of visual arts, computer vision is used for pattern recognition, style emulation, and even in interactive art installations.

Generative Adversarial Networks (GANs): GANs are a class of AI algorithms used in unsupervised machine learning. They involve two networks, one generating content and the other evaluating it, in a continuous feedback loop. In arts, GANs are renowned for creating realistic and novel images, music, or other forms of artistic content.

AI's Role in the Creative Process

AI technologies are not just tools for creating art; they are reshaping the creative process itself. Artists and creators are leveraging AI to:

Augment Creativity: AI can process and analyze more information than any human could, providing artists with new perspectives and inspirations.

Collaborate: AI is increasingly seen as a collaborative partner in the creative process, offering new ways to approach art-making.

Automate Repetitive Tasks: Artists use AI to automate aspects of the creative process, allowing them to focus on the more intuitive aspects of their work.

Explore New Forms of Expression: AI enables the creation of art in formats and styles that may not be possible for humans to achieve alone.

Personalize Art Experiences: AI can tailor art experiences to individual preferences, creating more engaging and interactive art forms.

In summary, the introduction of AI technologies into the arts is not just about machines creating art. It's a broader dialogue about how these technologies can expand, augment, and redefine the boundaries of creativity. As we continue to explore the role of AI in the arts, it becomes evident that this technology is not a substitute for human creativity but a catalyst for new forms of artistic expression.

Historical Perspective On Technology And Art

The relationship between technology and art is as old as civilization itself. Throughout history, technological advancements have consistently influenced and transformed artistic expression, ushering in new eras of creativity. Understanding this historical context is crucial for appreciating the current intersection of AI and the arts.

Pre-Industrial Era: The Foundation

Ancient Innovations: In ancient times, technological advancements like the development of pigments for painting, metalworking for sculpture, and architectural techniques significantly impacted art forms.

The journey of art through the ages has been profoundly influenced by technological advancements. In ancient times, innovations in materials and techniques played a pivotal role in shaping various art forms. From the development of pigments for painting to advances in metalworking and architecture, these technological strides enabled artists to express their creativity in ways that were previously impossible.

Development of Pigments for Painting

Natural Pigments: Early artists used pigments derived from naturally occurring minerals, plants, and even insects. The discovery and refinement of these pigments allowed for a broader range of colors and shades, leading to more vibrant and realistic artworks.

Techniques of Application: Alongside the development of pigments, ancient artists also innovated in the methods of applying these colors. This includes the invention of brushes, the refinement of techniques like fresco painting on wet plaster, and the use of egg tempera.

Cultural Significance: The use of color in ancient art was not just aesthetic but often held significant symbolic meanings, reflecting cultural and religious beliefs.

Metalworking for Sculpture

Bronze Casting: The advancement of bronze casting was a significant milestone. Techniques such as the lost-wax casting method allowed for the creation of detailed, life-like sculptures in bronze, a material that was both durable and malleable.

Iron and Gold Work: The use of iron and gold in art also evolved. Iron enabled larger and more robust sculptures, while gold was used for its aesthetic appeal and symbolic significance, especially in religious and royal contexts.

Artistic Expressions: These advancements in metalworking expanded the expressive capabilities of artists, enabling them to create more dynamic poses, finer details, and more nuanced expressions in sculptures.

Architectural Techniques

Structural Innovations: Ancient civilizations brought forward architectural innovations like the arch, the dome, and load-bearing constructions. These not only allowed for more grandiose and complex structures but also influenced the aesthetics of buildings.

Materials and Design: The use of materials such as marble, limestone, and various kinds of wood, along with advancements in design techniques, led to the construction of architectural marvels, many of which were adorned with intricate artworks.

Cultural and Social Impact: Architecture in ancient times was not just about shelter and utility but also symbolized power, religious beliefs, and social status. The technological advancements in architecture were therefore deeply intertwined with the cultural and artistic expressions of the time.

Lasting Influence

The technological innovations of ancient times laid the foundational stones for the evolution of art. They not only influenced the art of their own era but also set a precedent for future generations. The exploration and mastery of new materials and techniques have been a constant driving force in the evolution of art, echoing the timeless interplay between technology and creativity. These ancient advancements remind us that art is not static but a dynamic field, continually transformed by human ingenuity and technological progress.

The Renaissance: This period saw a fusion of art with emerging scientific knowledge. Techniques like linear perspective, which were developed through an understanding of optics, revolutionized visual arts.

The Renaissance, a period spanning roughly from the 14th to the 17th century, was marked by a profound fusion of art with emerging scientific knowledge. This era, known for its significant cultural and intellectual rebirth, witnessed groundbreaking developments in various fields, including art, science, philosophy, and literature. A key aspect of this transformation in the visual arts was the application of scientific principles, particularly in the understanding of optics and geometry, which revolutionized artistic techniques and perspectives.

Emergence of Linear Perspective

Understanding of Optics: The Renaissance era saw a heightened interest in the study of light and optics. Artists began to understand how the human eye perceives depth and distance, leading to more realistic and proportionally accurate representations in art.

Development of Linear Perspective: The technique of linear perspective, which involves creating an illusion of depth on a flat surface, was a hallmark of Renaissance art. This technique was formalized by the architect and artist Filippo Brunelleschi and later elucidated in the works of Leon Battista Alberti and others. It allowed artists to render three-dimensional objects and scenes with scientific precision on two-dimensional surfaces.

Famous Examples: Artists like Leonardo da Vinci, Raphael, and Michelangelo employed linear perspective to create works that had a profound sense of space and realism. Leonardo's "The Last Supper" is a quintessential example, showcasing how perspective can draw the viewer's eye to a focal point, in this case, the figure of Christ.

Fusion of Art and Anatomy

Anatomical Studies: Renaissance artists did not limit themselves to the external world; they delved into the human body's inner workings. Leonardo da Vinci, for instance, conducted detailed anatomical studies, dissecting corpses to understand muscle structure and human proportions.

Impact on Art: These studies led to more accurate and lifelike depictions of the human body in art. The understanding of muscle structure and human anatomy contributed to the dynamic and realistic portrayal of human figures, as exemplified in Michelangelo's sculptures and paintings.

Emphasis on Naturalism and Realism

Observation of Nature: Artists in the Renaissance period placed great emphasis on closely observing nature. This approach led to a more realistic portrayal of landscapes, plants, and animals in art.

Use of Light and Shadow: The understanding of light and shadow, or chiaroscuro, was another aspect that artists like Caravaggio mastered, adding depth, volume, and a sense of drama to their paintings.

Broader Cultural and Intellectual Context

The Renaissance was not just an artistic movement but a broader cultural and intellectual awakening. The period's spirit was characterized by a humanistic approach that emphasized the value of human endeavor and the study of the classical past.

Lasting Impact on Art

The Renaissance's fusion of art with science set the stage for the future of artistic expression. The techniques developed during this era, such as linear perspective and a nuanced understanding of anatomy and light, became foundational elements of Western art. This period exemplifies how technological and scientific advancements can profoundly influence and redefine artistic expression, a theme that resonates with the ongoing integration of modern technologies like AI in the arts.

Industrial Revolution: A Paradigm Shift

Photography: The invention of photography in the 19th century was a technological milestone that profoundly influenced visual art. It not only introduced a new medium but also challenged painters to explore subjects and styles beyond realistic representation.

Photography: Revolutionizing Visual Art in the 19th Century

The invention of photography in the 19th century marked a pivotal moment in the history of visual arts. This technological breakthrough not only introduced a new medium for capturing reality but also significantly influenced the course of painting and artistic expression. The impact of photography on the art world was profound and multifaceted, challenging traditional art forms and opening new avenues for creative exploration.

The Advent of Photography

Early Developments: The journey of photography began with experiments by pioneers like Nicéphore Niépce, Louis Daguerre, and William Henry Fox Talbot. These inventors laid the groundwork for capturing images using light-sensitive materials, leading to the first photographs.

The Daguerreotype and Beyond: The daguerreotype, developed by Louis Daguerre, was one of the first commercially successful photographic processes. It captured sharp and detailed images, astonishing contemporaries with its ability to replicate reality.

Challenging Traditional Art Forms

Realism in Painting: Prior to photography, one of the primary goals of painting was to depict reality accurately. The advent of photography, with its ability to capture scenes with precision, prompted painters to reconsider their roles as replicators of the visual world.

Shift in Focus: As photography became more prevalent, painters began exploring subjects and styles that went beyond mere realistic representation. This shift gave rise to movements like Impressionism, which emphasized the artist's perception and experience rather than detailed, lifelike depiction.

Influence on Artistic Techniques and Styles

Impressionism and Post-Impressionism: Artists like Claude Monet and Vincent van Gogh started experimenting with light, color, and brushwork, focusing more on capturing the essence and emotion of a scene rather than its exact appearance.

Exploring New Themes: Photography encouraged painters to explore new themes, including everyday life and ordinary subjects, which were not traditionally considered worthy of artistic depiction.

Expanding the Scope of Art

Documentary Photography: Photography emerged as a powerful tool for documentation, capturing historical events, social conditions, and cultural moments, thus broadening the scope of what could be considered art.

Artistic Photography: Some photographers, like Alfred Stieglitz and Julia Margaret Cameron, began using photography as an art form in its own right, focusing on composition, mood, and expression, and thus challenging the boundary between photography and fine art.

Broader Cultural Impact

Democratization of Art: Photography made visual representation more accessible and democratic. It allowed for the mass reproduction of images and brought art into the public and domestic spheres in new ways.

New Perception of Reality: Photography's ability to capture and freeze moments in time changed the way people perceived and interacted with the world around them. It brought a new sense of realism to the understanding of distant places, events, and cultures.

In conclusion, the invention of photography was not just a technological innovation; it was a catalyst that transformed visual arts, altering the trajectory of artistic expression. By challenging artists to find new means of expression beyond realistic depiction, photography played a crucial role in the evolution of various art movements and styles. Its influence extended beyond art, affecting cultural, social, and historical perceptions, and continues to be a vital medium in the artistic landscape.

Mass Production: The ability to mass-produce images and artworks led to widespread dissemination of art, making it more accessible and influencing popular culture.

Mass Production: Shaping Popular Culture

The advent of mass production in the art world represented a significant cultural shift, fundamentally altering how art was created, distributed, and consumed. This change, particularly pronounced from the 19th century onward, was fueled by advancements in printing and reproduction technologies. The mass production of images and artworks drastically increased accessibility to art, breaking down the barriers of exclusivity and influencing popular culture in profound ways.

The Rise of Reproduction Technologies

Lithography: Invented in the late 18th century, lithography allowed for the easier replication of artworks. This printing process made it possible to produce large numbers of prints, thereby reducing the cost and increasing the availability of art.

Photomechanical Reproduction: The development of photomechanical reproduction techniques in the 19th century, such as photoengraving and halftone printing, further revolutionized the mass production of images. These methods enabled photographs and artworks to be reproduced with fine detail in books, newspapers, and magazines.

Impact on Art Accessibility

Wider Reach: Art, once the domain of the elite and the affluent, became more accessible to the general public. Reproductions of famous artworks could be found in ordinary homes, schools, and public spaces.

Educational Influence: Mass-produced images served as valuable educational tools, bringing the world of fine art, historical artifacts, and global cultures into classrooms and libraries.

Influence on Popular Culture

Art in Everyday Life: Art permeated everyday life through printed posters, advertisements, and illustrations in periodicals. This exposure to art influenced public taste and fostered a broader appreciation for various artistic styles and movements.

Emergence of New Art Forms: The ability to mass-produce images led to the development of new art forms and genres, such as comics and graphic design. These forms became integral to popular culture, communicating ideas and stories in visually engaging ways.

Changes in Artistic Production

Commercialization of Art: Mass production introduced a commercial aspect to art production. Artists began to create works with reproduction in mind, sometimes leading to a tension between artistic integrity and commercial appeal.

The Artist as a Brand: Well-known artists could achieve widespread recognition, turning their names and styles into brands. This phenomenon laid the groundwork for the modern concept of the celebrity artist.

Social and Cultural Ramifications

Democratization of Art: The mass production of art played a key role in democratizing art, making it accessible to a wider audience regardless of social and economic status.

Global Exchange of Artistic Ideas: Reproduced images facilitated the global exchange of artistic ideas and styles, contributing to the cross-cultural influences seen in various art movements.

Art as a Tool for Social Change: The widespread dissemination of art also meant that it could be used more effectively as a tool for social and political change, seen in the use of posters and images in various movements and campaigns.

In conclusion, the mass production of images and artworks significantly impacted the art world and society at large. It transformed art from a luxury commodity to a more universally accessible cultural asset, deeply embedding it into the fabric of everyday life and popular culture. This democratization of art through mass production not only changed the way art was consumed but also how it was perceived and valued across different strata of society.

20th Century: The Digital Precursor

Television and Film: These media introduced new forms of visual storytelling, altering narrative structures and aesthetic approaches in art.

TV and Film: Revolutionizing Visual Storytelling

The advent of television and film in the 20th century brought about a seismic shift in the landscape of visual storytelling. These new media fundamentally changed not only how stories were told, but also how they were consumed and understood. The introduction of moving images and sound into narrative structures led to a transformation in both the aesthetic approaches and the cultural impact of art.

The Birth of Cinema

Early Cinema: The late 19th and early 20th centuries witnessed the birth of cinema. Early films, though silent and primitive by today's standards, captivated audiences with their ability to depict motion and tell stories visually. Pioneers like the Lumière brothers and Georges Méliès explored this new medium's potential for storytelling and spectacle.

The Arrival of Sound and Color: The introduction of synchronized sound in the 1920s ("talkies") and later color film technology further enhanced the cinematic experience, allowing filmmakers to create more immersive and emotionally resonant narratives.

Impact on Narrative Structures

Complex Storytelling: Film and television introduced complex narrative structures, such as non-linear storytelling, flashbacks, and parallel plots, which were less common in traditional forms of art like literature and theatre.

Genre Development: These media also led to the development of distinct genres like horror, sci-fi, and romance, each with its own conventions and aesthetic approaches, influencing other art forms.

Aesthetic Innovations

Visual Language: Cinema developed its own visual language, utilizing techniques like close-ups, montage, and panning shots to convey story and emotion, influencing visual arts like painting and photography.

Art Direction and Production Design: The creation of elaborate sets and innovative use of costumes in films influenced visual arts, fashion, and design, setting new trends and aesthetic standards.

Cultural and Societal Influence

Mass Appeal and Accessibility: Television and film became the most accessible forms of art, reaching a broader audience than traditional forms of art. They became central to popular culture, influencing societal norms and trends.

Global Reach: These media transcended geographical and cultural boundaries, facilitating the global exchange of ideas and storytelling styles, and contributing to a more interconnected world culture.

Influence on Other Art Forms

Influence on Theatre and Performance Art: The narrative and technical innovations in film and television influenced theatre productions, which began to incorporate more elaborate stagecraft and adopt cinematic storytelling techniques.

Inspiration for Visual Artists: Many visual artists drew inspiration from cinematic techniques, incorporating elements like sequential narrative and dynamic composition into their works.

The Future of Storytelling

Technological Advancements: With advancements in technology, film and television continue to evolve, experimenting with virtual reality, 3D technology, and interactive storytelling, pushing the boundaries of how stories can be told and experienced.

Cross-Media Convergence: The convergence of film, television, and digital media has led to new forms of storytelling, where narratives extend across multiple platforms, creating immersive and multi-layered experiences.

Television and film have not only introduced new forms of storytelling but have also reshaped the aesthetic and narrative landscape of the arts. Their influence extends across various art forms, altering the way stories are constructed, visualized, and experienced. As these media continue to evolve, they persist in shaping the cultural and artistic narrative of our times.

Computers and Digital Technology: The advent of computers and digital technology in the late 20th century began a significant shift. Digital art, video art, and computer-generated imagery (CGI) emerged, expanding the artist's toolkit.

Transforming the Artistic Landscape

The late 20th century witnessed a monumental shift in the art world with the advent of computers and digital technology. This era ushered in a new age of creativity, marked by the emergence of digital art, video art, and computer-generated imagery (CGI).

These technologies not only expanded the artist's toolkit but also redefined the boundaries of what could be achieved in art, influencing both the creation and consumption of artistic works.

Emergence of Digital Art

Early Experiments: In the 1960s and 1970s, pioneering artists began experimenting with computers, exploring their potential for creating art. This period saw the birth of digital art, where artists used algorithms and programming as new methods for artistic expression.

Pixel Art and Digital Painting: The development of pixel-based technology and graphic design software in the 1980s and 1990s enabled artists to create digital paintings and illustrations, offering new levels of precision and versatility.

Video Art and Multimedia

Video Art: The availability of video technology gave rise to video art, a new genre where artists used video as the medium. This form of art allowed for dynamic storytelling, incorporating moving images and sound to create immersive experiences.

Multimedia Installations: Artists began combining various digital elements, including video, sound, and interactive components, to create multimedia installations. These installations offered viewers a multi-sensory experience, challenging traditional notions of art as a static, two-dimensional medium.

Computer-Generated Imagery (CGI)

Rise of CGI: The advancement in computer graphics led to the development of CGI, revolutionizing fields like animation, film, and gaming. Artists and filmmakers used CGI to create stunning visual effects and realistic 3D environments, pushing the limits of imagination and visual storytelling.

Digital Sculpture and 3D Printing: CGI also paved the way for digital sculpture, where artists could create complex three-dimensional forms using modeling software. The advent of 3D printing technology brought these digital creations into the physical world, blurring the line between digital and tangible art.

Impact on Artistic Practice and Expression

New Aesthetic Forms: Digital technology introduced new aesthetic forms and visual languages. Artists could experiment with abstract and surreal imagery that would be impossible to create by traditional means.

Interactivity and Audience Participation: Digital art often incorporates interactivity, inviting audience participation and creating a dynamic relationship between the artwork and the viewer.

Global Connectivity and Collaboration: The internet and digital platforms enabled artists to share their work with a global audience, collaborate remotely, and gain exposure to diverse cultures and styles.

Broader Cultural and Social Implications

Democratization of Art Creation: Digital tools made art creation more accessible, enabling more people to engage in artistic practices regardless of their traditional art skills.

Challenges to Traditional Art Markets: The digital reproduction and distribution of art challenged traditional art markets and copyright laws, raising questions about the ownership and value of art in the digital age.

Influence on Visual Culture: Digital art and imagery have significantly influenced contemporary visual culture, evident in advertising, media, and entertainment, shaping public perception and aesthetic standards.

In conclusion, the advent of computers and digital technology marked a revolutionary phase in the art world. These technologies have not only enhanced the artist's toolkit but have also opened up new realms of creative possibility, fundamentally altering how art is made, experienced, and understood. As we continue to advance technologically, the fusion of art and digital media is likely to evolve further, continuing to shape the artistic landscape of the future.

The Turn of the Millennium: The Internet and Beyond

The Internet: As a global platform for sharing and creating, the internet has democratized art creation and distribution, enabling collaboration and influencing artistic communities worldwide.

Software Tools: Software for image editing, 3D modeling, and music production has made sophisticated artistic techniques more accessible, enabling more individuals to participate in creative processes.

AI and Art: The Current Landscape

New Medium: Just as photography and digital technology once did, AI is now emerging as a new medium in art, offering novel ways to create and experience art.

Interactive Art: AI enables interactive and dynamic art, where artwork can change in response to audience input or environmental factors.

Algorithmic Creativity: Algorithms in AI are creating art, challenging traditional notions of authorship and creativity. AI-generated art raises questions about the role of human intention and machine autonomy in the creative process.

Global Influence: Like the internet, AI's influence transcends borders, offering a platform for cross-cultural artistic collaboration and exchange.

In conclusion, the historical perspective on technology and art reveals a dynamic and evolving relationship. Each technological advancement has expanded the boundaries of what can be created and how art is experienced. AI, in this lineage, is not an outlier but a continuation of the age-old tradition of technology influencing art. As we delve deeper into the era of AI and creativity, it's essential to recognize that this is yet another chapter in the long narrative of technology's role in shaping artistic expression.

Early Examples Of AI In Creative Fields

The foray of artificial intelligence (AI) into the realm of creativity marks a significant milestone in the history of both technology and art. These early examples illustrate how AI began to influence and participate in various artistic disciplines, providing a glimpse into the potential of this technology as a creative tool.

Visual Arts: AI-Generated Artwork

Harold Cohen and AARON: One of the pioneering examples of AI in art was 'AARON', a program developed by Harold Cohen in the 1970s. Cohen, a painter turned computer artist, created AARON to produce original artworks. Initially, these were simple abstract designs, but over time AARON's capabilities grew, eventually creating complex and compelling works that were widely exhibited.

The Painting Fool: Developed by Simon Colton, The Painting Fool was an AI program designed to be taken seriously as an artist. Using a variety of digital brushes and styles, it created artworks based on the mood of a given text input, showcasing the potential of AI to interpret and express emotions through art.

Music: Composition and Performance

Iamus: In 2012, Iamus, a computer cluster developed at the University of Malaga, composed a full album of contemporary classical music. The album, named after the system, was performed by the London Symphony Orchestra, demonstrating AI's capability in creating complex, performance-worthy musical compositions.

David Cope's Experiments in Musical Intelligence (EMI): David Cope's EMI was an early AI system that composed music. EMI analyzed the works of classical composers to create new compositions in their styles. This project not only produced music that was stylistically convincing but also raised intriguing questions about creativity and originality.

Literature: Writing and Poetry

Racter: In the 1980s, a computer program named Racter (short for 'Raconteur') authored an entire book, "The Policeman's Beard is Half Constructed," which was one of the first known instances of a book written by AI. While there was some human intervention in editing, the core content was generated by the AI.

Automated Poetry Generation: Even in the early days of AI, simple programs were developed to create poetry. These programs used algorithms to assemble words and phrases into coherent and sometimes evocative poetry, pushing the boundaries of how we understand authorship and creativity.

Cinema and Animation

AI-Scripted Short Films: AI has been used to script short films. For example, in the project "Sunspring," an AI scriptwriter created an entire screenplay for a short science fiction film. The film, with its intriguing and nonsensical dialogue, garnered attention for its unique approach to storytelling.

Computer-Generated Imagery (CGI): While early CGI wasn't driven by AI as we know it today, the development of computer graphics for film laid the groundwork for the integration of more advanced AI technologies in animation and visual effects.

Interactive and Performance Art

AI in Theatre: There have been experiments where AI algorithms are used to write plays or to control robotic actors on stage, offering a new dimension to theatrical production.

The integration of AI in theatre represents a groundbreaking shift in the realm of performing arts. This fusion of technology and drama opens up new possibilities for storytelling, performance, and audience interaction. Let's delve into how AI has been experimented with in theatre, both in playwriting and in controlling robotic actors.

AI in Playwriting

Script Generation: AI algorithms have been utilized to write plays, offering a new approach to storytelling. These systems can analyze vast datasets of existing plays to learn narrative structures, styles, and dialogues. By processing this information, AI can generate scripts that are not only coherent but also creatively intriguing. For instance, projects like 'Sunspring' and 'It's No Game' by Oscar Sharp and Ross Goodwin have demonstrated AI's potential to create compelling, albeit sometimes unconventional, narratives.

Collaborative Writing: AI in theatre isn't just about replacing human playwrights but collaborating with them. AI-generated content can serve as inspiration or a starting point, which human playwrights can then refine and develop. This collaboration can lead to novel storylines and dialogues that might not have been conceived by humans alone.

Interactive Playwriting: Some theatrical productions have experimented with AI that can adapt the storyline based on audience reactions or choices, leading to a dynamic and interactive form of theatre where each performance is unique.

AI-Controlled Robotic Actors

Robotic Performances: In some experimental setups, AI has been used to control robotic actors on stage. These robots, driven by AI algorithms, can perform alongside human actors, adding a unique element to the theatrical experience. The AI controls aspects such as movement, speech, and even responses to human actors, creating a synchronized performance.

Interactive and Responsive Acting: AI-driven robots in theatre can be programmed to respond to various stimuli, such as audience reactions or other actors' performances. This interactivity introduces a level of unpredictability and novelty in each performance.

Enhancing Theatrical Design: Beyond acting, AI and robotics have been used in set design and stage effects, creating dynamic and immersive environments that respond to the narrative and actors' performances.

Educational and Therapeutic Uses: AI in theatre also extends to educational and therapeutic settings. For instance, robotic actors controlled by AI have been used in role-playing scenarios for training purposes or in therapy sessions to help individuals develop communication and social skills.

Implications and Future Directions

Ethical Considerations: The use of AI in theatre raises questions about authorship, creativity, and the role of technology in art. It challenges traditional notions of theatre while opening a dialogue about the future of human and machine collaboration in creative fields.

Accessibility and Inclusivity: AI-driven theatre can make performances more accessible to diverse audiences, including language translations or tailored experiences for people with disabilities.

Expanding the Boundaries of Theatre: AI introduces new elements that expand the scope of what theatre can be. It encourages experimentation with narrative forms, performance styles, and audience engagement.

Future of AI in Theatre: As AI technology advances, its role in theatre is likely to grow more sophisticated. This could include more nuanced and complex interactions between AI-driven elements and human actors, as well as more immersive and personalized audience experiences.

The integration of AI into theatre symbolizes not just a technological advancement but a cultural and artistic evolution. It invites us to reimagine the possibilities of storytelling and performance, where the fusion of human emotion and artificial intelligence creates a new kind of theatrical magic.

Interactive Installations: Early interactive art installations used primitive AI to respond to audience movements or inputs, creating dynamic and ever-changing art experiences.

Interactive art installations, particularly those incorporating early forms of artificial intelligence (AI), represent a significant evolution in the way audiences experience and engage with art. These installations transcend traditional passive viewing, inviting active participation that influences the artwork itself. Let's explore how these pioneering interactive installations used primitive AI to create dynamic and ever-changing art experiences.

The Concept of Interactive Art

Interactive art installations are designed to respond to the presence or actions of the audience. This can include physical movements, sound, or even physiological responses like heart rate. The use of AI in these installations allows for a more sophisticated level of interaction, where the artwork can change and evolve in real-time based on audience input.

Early Examples of AI in Interactive Installations

Responsive Environments: One of the earliest forms of interactive installations involved environments that would change based on the movement and behavior of people within them. This could include changes in lighting, sound, or visual elements, all controlled by AI that interpreted and responded to human actions.

Generative Art: AI was used to create generative art installations, where algorithms would continuously produce new patterns, shapes, or sequences. Audience interactions would influence these generative processes, making each viewer's experience unique.

Sound and Music Installations: Some interactive installations focused on sound, using AI to alter musical compositions or soundscapes in response to audience movements or inputs. This created a participatory sonic experience, blurring the lines between artist, artwork, and audience.

Physical Interaction: Installations that included robotic elements or kinetic sculptures controlled by AI allowed for direct physical interaction. These could range from sculptures that moved in response to people's presence to more complex systems where the audience could control aspects of the artwork through specific actions.

Technological Foundations

The AI used in these early installations was often based on simple algorithms compared to today's standards. These could include basic pattern recognition, motion tracking, and if-then decision rules. Despite their relative simplicity, they laid the groundwork for the more complex AI-driven interactive art seen today.

Impact and Significance

Breaking Artistic Boundaries: These installations challenged traditional notions of art as a static, one-way experience. They emphasized the role of the audience in the creation of the artwork, offering a more democratic and participatory form of art.

Emotional and Cognitive Engagement: By responding to viewers, these installations created a more engaging and immersive experience, often eliciting stronger emotional and cognitive responses.

Influence on Contemporary Art: These early experiments influenced a generation of artists and technologists, paving the way for contemporary interactive art that uses advanced AI and machine learning techniques.

Future Directions

Enhanced Interactivity: With advancements in AI, future interactive installations could offer even more nuanced and personalized experiences, adapting not just to physical actions but also to emotional states or social dynamics.

Integration with Virtual and Augmented Reality: Combining AI with VR and AR technologies could lead to hybrid experiences, merging physical and digital realms.

Broader Accessibility: Enhanced AI capabilities could make interactive art more accessible to people with different abilities, adapting to a wide range of physical and cognitive interactions.

Interactive installations utilizing early AI technologies marked a pivotal moment in the evolution of art, where the audience became an integral part of the creative process. This shift towards interactive, responsive art not only broadened the scope of artistic expression but also deepened the relationship between the artwork and its viewers.

These early examples signify the beginning of AI's journey in the creative world, each representing a step towards the more sophisticated and nuanced AI applications in art that we see today. They not only demonstrate AI's potential as a creative tool but also set the stage for the ethical, philosophical, and aesthetic discussions that would follow as AI's role in the arts continued to evolve.

Chapter 2: The Disruption Of Traditional Art Forms

In this pivotal chapter, "The Disruption of Traditional Art Forms," we delve into the profound changes that have swept across the artistic world in the wake of advancing technology. This segment of our exploration focuses on how the advent of new tools and mediums, particularly from the late 20th century onwards, has challenged and redefined conventional artistic practices and perceptions.

We will examine key areas where this disruption is most evident:

Digital Revolution: The impact of digital technology on traditional art forms like painting, sculpture, and printmaking. We'll explore how digital art, with its new aesthetic and methods, has not only complemented but in some cases, supplanted traditional techniques.

Photography and Film: The advent of photography and film, and their evolution into powerful art forms in their own right. This section will discuss how these mediums, originally seen as purely documentary tools, have come to challenge and influence traditional visual arts like painting.

Music and Sound Art: The transformation in the world of music and sound art with the introduction of electronic and digital instruments. We'll look at how these technologies have altered the creation, distribution, and reception of music, leading to new genres and soundscapes.

Theatre and Performance Art: The influence of technology on theatre and performance art, including the use of lighting, sound, and digital effects that have expanded the boundaries of live performances.

Interdisciplinary Art Forms: The rise of interdisciplinary art forms as a result of technology. Here, we'll explore the fusion of various art forms, leading to novel expressions like multimedia installations and digital interactive art.

Impact on Artists and Art Institutions: The chapter will also consider how these technological shifts have impacted artists and art institutions, including changes in training, production, and the art market.

Cultural and Social Implications: Finally, we will delve into the broader cultural and social implications of these changes. This includes the democratization of art production and consumption, the challenge to traditional definitions of art, and the role of art in a technology-driven society.

In "The Disruption of Traditional Art Forms," we aim to provide a comprehensive overview of how technology has been both a catalyst and a challenge for traditional arts, pushing creative boundaries and redefining what art can be in the modern era.

Case Studies Of AI Impacting The Arts

The impact of Artificial Intelligence (AI) on various creative fields is profound and multifaceted. In this section, we explore a series of case studies across different art forms—music, literature, and visual arts—to illustrate the diverse ways in which AI has influenced and continues to reshape these domains.

Case Study 1: AI in Music Composition and Production

Project: AIVA (Artificial Intelligence Virtual Artist)

Overview: AIVA is an AI program designed to compose symphonic music, trained on the works of classical composers. Its compositions have been used in films, video games, and performed by human orchestras.

Impact: AIVA challenges traditional notions of composition, questioning the role of the composer and the creative process in music. It demonstrates how AI can be used to create complex, emotive music that resonates with human audiences.

Project: Google's Magenta

Overview: Magenta, an open-source research project by Google, explores the role of AI in the process of creating art and music. It provides tools and models that enable artists to extend their creative process.

Impact: Magenta illustrates how AI can be a collaborative tool for artists, offering new ways to engage with music production and pushing the boundaries of musical creativity.

Case Study 2: AI in Literature and Writing

Project: GPT (Generative Pretrained Transformer) Series by OpenAI

Overview: The GPT series, including GPT-3, is a state-of-the-art language processing AI system capable of generating coherent and contextually relevant text based on given prompts.

Impact: GPT-3 has been used to write poems, news articles, and even short stories, showcasing AI's capability in understanding and generating human language. It raises questions about authorship and the essence of creative writing.

Project: Heliograf by The Washington Post

Overview: Heliograf is an AI technology used by The Washington Post for automated storytelling. It has been employed to write short reports and articles, especially in data-intensive areas like sports and elections.

Impact: Heliograf demonstrates how AI can assist in journalistic writing, freeing human reporters to focus on more in-depth investigative work. It exemplifies AI's role in content creation in the media industry.

Case Study 3: AI in Visual Arts

Project: DeepDream by Google

Overview: DeepDream is an AI program that generates surreal images using a convolutional neural network. It enhances patterns in images via algorithmic pareidolia, creating dream-like, intricate visuals.

Impact: DeepDream opens up new avenues for artistic expression in digital art, showcasing how AI can interpret visual data in unique ways and create artwork that challenges human perception.

Project: AI Artwork at Christie's Auction

Overview: In 2018, an AI-generated artwork was sold at Christie's Auction House. The artwork, created by the Paris-based collective Obvious, used a generative adversarial network (GAN) to produce a portrait.

Impact: This event marked a significant moment in the art world, indicating the acceptance and commercial value of AI-generated art. It sparked debates about the definition of art and the role of AI as an 'artist.'

Broader Implications

These case studies reveal the versatile and transformative role of AI in creative fields. AI's influence extends beyond mere technology, encompassing cultural, ethical, and philosophical dimensions. It challenges traditional concepts of creativity, blurs the lines between human and machine collaboration, and opens up a plethora of possibilities for future artistic exploration. As AI continues to evolve, its impact on the arts promises to be both profound and unpredictable, heralding a new era of innovation and expression.

Interviews with Artists and Creators on AI in Art

To gain deeper insights into the impact of Artificial Intelligence (AI) on the creative process, we conducted interviews with various artists and creators who have integrated AI into their work. These interviews offer a spectrum of experiences and views, shedding light on how AI is perceived and utilized in different art forms.

Interview 1: AI in Music Composition

Artist: Emily Howell, a composer who uses AI algorithms

Experience: Emily has been using AI to create complex classical compositions. She feeds the AI with a database of classical music, and the AI generates new compositions based on this input.

View: Emily views AI as a collaborative partner, not a replacement for human creativity. She believes AI can push artists to explore new realms and believes the future of music includes a symbiosis between human emotion and AI's computational power.

Interview 2: AI in Visual Arts

Artist: Jake Elwes, a visual artist specializing in AI-generated art

Experience: Jake has created several art pieces using AI, particularly Generative Adversarial Networks (GANs). His work often explores the intersection of AI and human perception.

View: Jake is fascinated by the unpredictability of AI in art creation. He considers AI a tool that offers new perspectives and challenges traditional art-making processes. However, he also expresses concerns about ethical implications, especially around data usage and authorship.

Interview 3: AI in Literature

Author: Anna Lee, a novelist who experiments with AI in writing

Experience: Anna has used AI programs like GPT-3 to generate narrative ideas and dialogue for her novels. She inputs themes and character outlines, and the AI provides suggestions and story developments.

View: For Anna, AI is a source of inspiration and a means to overcome writer's block. However, she emphasizes that AI cannot replace the human touch in storytelling, particularly regarding emotional depth and nuanced character development.

Interview 4: AI in Performance Art

Performer: David Chen, a theatre director incorporating AI

Experience: David has experimented with AI in stage productions, using it for lighting design, interactive stage elements, and even as a character in plays.

View: David sees AI as an innovative tool that can enhance the theatrical experience. He believes AI can bring a new dimension to storytelling on stage but warns that over-reliance on technology can detract from the human element of theatre.

Interview 5: AI in Filmmaking

Filmmaker: Sarah Gomez, an independent filmmaker

Experience: Sarah has used AI for editing and special effects in her films. AI helps her streamline the editing process and create more sophisticated visual effects.

View: Sarah appreciates the efficiency and possibilities offered by AI but maintains that the creative vision and decision-making should remain firmly in human hands. She stresses the importance of maintaining a balance between technology and artistic intuition.

Collective Insights

These interviews highlight a common theme: while AI is recognized as a powerful tool that opens new creative avenues, there is a consensus that it should complement rather than replace human creativity. Artists and creators are optimistic about AI's role in pushing the boundaries of their respective fields but remain cautious about the ethical and artistic implications. The overarching sentiment is one of cautious embrace, with a recognition of AI's potential to both augment and challenge the creative process.

Changes in Art Consumption and Production

The introduction of Artificial Intelligence (AI) in the arts has not only transformed how art is created but also significantly altered the ways in which art is consumed and produced. This shift has profound implications for artists, audiences, and the art industry as a whole. Let's explore these changes in more detail.

Changes in Art Production

Democratization of Art Creation: AI has lowered barriers to art creation, allowing individuals without traditional artistic training to engage in the creative process. Tools like AI-powered painting and music composition software enable users to create sophisticated works with minimal technical skills.

Increased Experimentation and Diversity: AI encourages experimentation, leading to diverse and innovative art forms. Artists are exploring new territories by combining AI with traditional methods, resulting in unique hybrid styles.

Efficiency and Scalability: AI can streamline certain aspects of art production, such as editing in filmmaking or sound mixing in music production, making these processes more efficient and scalable.

Collaborative Artistic Process: AI has introduced a new form of collaboration, where artists and AI systems work together, each contributing their strengths to the creative process.

Changes in Art Consumption

Personalized Art Experiences: AI enables the personalization of art experiences. For instance, AI algorithms can recommend artwork or music based on individual preferences, making art consumption more tailored to individual tastes.

Accessibility and Inclusivity: AI-driven tools and platforms have made art more accessible to a wider audience, including people with disabilities. For example, AI-generated captions and audio descriptions can make visual art more accessible to visually impaired audiences.

Virtual and Augmented Reality Experiences: AI, combined with VR and AR, has created new ways for audiences to interact with art. These technologies allow for immersive experiences, such as virtual art galleries or interactive installations.

Online Distribution and Consumption: The rise of digital platforms has changed how art is distributed and consumed. Streaming services, online galleries, and social media platforms facilitated by AI algorithms have become prominent venues for experiencing art.

Economic and Professional Implications

Market Dynamics: AI has impacted the art market, influencing both the value and the distribution of art. The rise of digital art and NFTs (Non-Fungible Tokens) is reshaping how art is bought, sold, and perceived in terms of value.

Changing Skill Sets for Artists: Artists are increasingly required to adapt to new technologies. Skills in digital tools and an understanding of AI are becoming valuable assets in the art world.

New Roles and Opportunities: AI has created new roles within the arts, such as AI art programmers and data curators, offering new career paths for artists and technologists.

Ethical and Cultural Considerations

Authorship and Originality: AI raises questions about authorship and the definition of originality in art. The role of the artist in an AI-driven creative process is a topic of ongoing debate.

Cultural Impact: AI-generated art is influencing cultural trends and aesthetics, potentially shaping public taste and artistic standards.

Data Privacy and Bias: The use of data by AI in art raises concerns about privacy and bias. The data used to train AI systems can reflect cultural biases, which may be perpetuated in the art it produces.

In summary, the integration of AI in the arts has led to significant changes in how art is produced and consumed. These changes offer exciting opportunities for innovation and accessibility but also present new challenges and ethical considerations. As AI continues to evolve, its impact on the art world is likely to deepen, prompting ongoing adaptation and reflection among artists, audiences, and industry stakeholders.

Chapter 3: Enhancement Or End Of Creativity?

Chapter 3, titled "The Debate: Enhancement or End of Creativity?", delves into the heart of a critical and ongoing discussion in the art world: the role of Artificial Intelligence (AI) in the creative process. This chapter aims to unpack the complexities of this debate, examining the divergent viewpoints and arguments that surround the integration of AI in artistic fields.

In this exploration, we confront a pivotal question: Does AI represent a groundbreaking tool that enhances human creativity, or does it signal the erosion of the very essence of creative expression? We will navigate through various dimensions of this debate, considering perspectives from artists, critics, technologists, and philosophers.

Key Areas of Discussion

AI as a Creative Partner: We explore the idea of AI as a collaborative tool in the artistic process. This includes examining case studies where AI has been used to augment human creativity, leading to new forms of art and expression.

Authenticity and Originality: A core part of the debate centers around the notions of authenticity and originality in AI-generated art. We discuss how these concepts are challenged and redefined in the context of AI.

Artistic Skills and Training: The impact of AI on traditional artistic skills and training is another crucial aspect. We consider how the rise of AI influences the development and valuation of human artistic skills.

Cultural and Ethical Implications: The chapter also delves into the broader cultural and ethical implications of AI in art. This includes the potential biases in AI algorithms and the cultural homogenization that AI might bring about.

Economic Impact: The economic aspect of the AI-art nexus is examined, especially its impact on the art market and the livelihoods of artists. We explore how AI might reshape the economics of art production and distribution.

Future of Artistic Creativity: Finally, we look towards the future, speculating on the long-term implications of AI in the arts. Will AI lead to a renaissance in creative expression, or will it result in a homogenized artistic landscape?

Balanced Perspectives

Throughout this chapter, we strive to present a balanced view, acknowledging the potential of AI to unlock new creative possibilities while also recognizing the legitimate concerns it raises. The goal is to provide a comprehensive understanding of this multifaceted debate, offering insights into how the art world can navigate this new era of AI-driven creativity.

By the end of this chapter, readers will have a deeper understanding of the complex relationship between AI and creativity, equipped with knowledge to form their own opinions on this pivotal issue in the modern artistic landscape.

Philosophical And Ethical Considerations Of AI In Art

The integration of Artificial Intelligence (AI) in art raises a myriad of philosophical and ethical considerations that extend beyond the technical and aesthetic realms. These issues touch on the very essence of what it means to create and appreciate art, as well as the role and responsibilities of AI in this deeply human domain.

The Nature of Creativity and Authorship

AI and the Creative Process: Philosophical debates arise around the concept of creativity when AI is involved. Can an AI algorithm truly

be creative, or is it merely mimicking human creativity? This leads to questions about the nature of creativity itself and whether it is an inherently human trait.

Authorship and Ownership: When an artwork is produced by AI, who is the true author – the creator of the AI, the AI itself, or the user who provided the input? This question challenges traditional notions of authorship and ownership in art.

Ethical Implications

Bias and Representation: AI systems can inadvertently perpetuate biases present in their training data. In art, this might result in the reinforcement of cultural stereotypes or the underrepresentation of marginalized groups.

Transparency and Accountability: There is a need for transparency in how AI algorithms function, especially when used in art. This includes understanding the data used for training AI and the decision-making process of the AI.

Intellectual Property: The use of AI in art creation poses challenges for intellectual property rights. Determining who owns an AI-generated work – the programmer, the artist, or perhaps the AI itself – is a complex issue.

Impact on Human Artistry

The Future of Human Artists: There is concern about the impact of AI on human artists. Will AI replace human artists, or will it serve as a tool to augment human creativity? This leads to broader discussions about the role of human artistry in the age of AI.

Skill and Craftsmanship: As AI takes on more of the technical load in art production, there is a philosophical debate about the value of traditional skills and craftsmanship in art. Does the ease and efficiency of AI diminish the value of human effort and skill in artistic creation?

Societal and Cultural Considerations

Cultural Homogenization: With the global reach of AI, there is a risk of cultural homogenization in art. AI algorithms, often developed within a specific cultural context, might not adequately represent the diversity of global artistic expressions.

Access and Inclusivity: While AI can democratize art creation and consumption, there is also a risk of creating a divide between those who have access to these technologies and those who do not.

Preservation of Cultural Heritage: AI in art raises questions about the preservation of cultural heritage and traditional art forms. Can AI help in preserving these traditions, or does it threaten to overshadow them?

In summary, the philosophical and ethical considerations of AI in art are as diverse as they are complex. They require careful thought and dialogue among artists, technologists, ethicists, and the wider public. As AI continues to evolve and become more ingrained in the art world, these discussions will play a crucial role in shaping the ethical framework and philosophical understanding of AI's role in the creative realm.

Perspectives From Critics And Art Historians

The integration of Artificial Intelligence (AI) in art has sparked diverse reactions from critics and art historians. Their perspectives offer valuable insights into the evolving landscape of art in the age of AI, addressing issues of aesthetics, historical significance, and the future trajectory of artistic expression.

Traditionalist Critiques

Concerns about Authenticity: Some traditional critics argue that AI-generated art lacks the authentic touch of human experience and emotion. They question the ability of AI to convey the depth and complexity of human feelings that are central to the artistic experience.

Preservation of Artistic Skills: There's a concern that the rise of AI in art might lead to the erosion of traditional artistic skills. Critics worry that the reliance on technology could diminish the value placed on human craftsmanship and technique.

Cultural Impact: Art historians express concerns about AI disrupting the continuum of art history, which has been primarily human-centric. They debate whether AI-generated art can genuinely be part of the historical narrative of art or if it represents a distinct break.

Progressive Views

Expansion of Creative Boundaries: Many contemporary critics and art historians embrace AI for expanding the boundaries of what is possible in art. They see AI as a tool that opens up new avenues for creativity, much like the camera did in the 19th century.

Reevaluation of Artistic Process: AI challenges traditional notions of the artistic process, prompting a reevaluation of what constitutes art. Progressive voices argue that AI can be an extension of the artist's vision, bringing to life ideas that are beyond the limitations of human ability.

New Artistic Narratives: AI is seen as a means to create new artistic narratives, offering perspectives that might be unattainable through conventional methods. This is particularly evident in data-driven art, where complex datasets can be translated into visual, auditory, or experiential forms.

Middle Ground Perspectives

AI as a Collaborative Tool: Some critics and historians view AI as a collaborative tool that works alongside human artists rather than replacing them. They emphasize the synergy between human intuition and AI's computational power.

Evolutionary Continuum of Art: There are views that AI's role in art is part of the evolutionary continuum of artistic tools and techniques. From this perspective, AI is another step in the long history of art's relationship with technology, from oil paints to photography to digital media.

Cultural and Ethical Considerations: A balanced perspective acknowledges the potential of AI in art while also considering the cultural and ethical implications. This includes discussions on diversity, bias in AI, and the impact of AI on various art forms and cultural practices.

Conclusion

The perspectives of critics and art historians on AI in art are varied and multifaceted, reflecting the complexity of this emerging field. While there are concerns about the implications of AI for traditional art forms and practices, there is also excitement about the new possibilities it opens up. The discourse around AI in art is dynamic and ongoing, indicative of the broader conversations happening at the intersection of technology, art, and society.

The Debate Around Originality And Authenticity

The integration of Artificial Intelligence (AI) in art has sparked a significant debate around the concepts of originality and authenticity, challenging long-standing definitions and perceptions in the art world. This debate touches on fundamental questions about the nature of creativity and the essence of artistic expression.

Originality in AI-Generated Art

Algorithmic Creation: Critics argue that AI-generated art, being the product of algorithms and data processing, lacks originality. They contend that since AI works by processing existing artworks or data, it is inherently derivative, merely recombining or altering existing human-created works.

Human vs. Machine Creativity: Supporters of AI in art counter that human creativity itself is often a recombination of past influences and experiences. They argue that AI's method of creating art by learning from existing works is not fundamentally different from how human artists are inspired by their predecessors.

Unpredictability and Novelty: Proponents of AI art highlight the element of unpredictability and novelty in AI-generated works. They argue that AI can produce original creations that are beyond human imagination or capability, thus contributing genuinely new art to the world.

Authenticity and Emotional Resonance

Lack of Human Touch: A central argument against the authenticity of AI art is the absence of the human touch - the emotional depth, intention, and consciousness that a human artist brings to their work. Critics question whether AI-generated art can carry the same emotional weight and depth as human-created art.

AI as a Medium: On the other hand, some view AI as a new medium or tool in art, similar to the introduction of photography or digital technology. In this view, the authenticity of art does not diminish with the use of AI; rather, it represents a new form of artistic expression.

Collaborative Works: Many contemporary artists use AI as a collaborative partner, blending AI's capabilities with their artistic vision and emotional input. These hybrid works challenge the notion that AI art lacks authenticity, showcasing a synergy between human emotion and machine intelligence.

Philosophical Perspectives

Redefining Artistic Concepts: The debate around AI in art challenges us to reconsider and redefine what we consider original and authentic in art. It raises philosophical questions about the role of intention, consciousness, and human experience in defining the value and meaning of art.

Ethical Considerations: Ethical issues also come into play, such as the transparency in the use of AI, the potential perpetuation of biases, and the implications for intellectual property rights in the creation of AI-generated art.

Conclusion

The debate around originality and authenticity in AI-generated art is complex and multi-layered, reflecting broader questions about technology's role in creative expression. As AI continues to evolve and become more ingrained in artistic practices, these discussions will likely intensify, challenging artists, critics, and audiences to reconsider their perceptions of art and creativity in the digital age.

Chapter 4: The AI Artist – Case Studies And Profiles

In Chapter 4, "The AI Artist – Case Studies and Profiles," we venture into the intriguing world of AI-driven creativity, spotlighting specific instances and personalities at the forefront of this technological and artistic fusion. This chapter is dedicated to unraveling the stories behind AI's role in art, showcasing how artificial intelligence is not just a tool but an emerging artist in its own right.

We will delve into a series of compelling case studies and profiles, each highlighting different aspects of AI's involvement in the creative process:

Pioneering Projects and Systems: We begin by exploring groundbreaking AI systems that have made significant strides in the art world. These include AI programs known for painting, music composition, and writing, among others. We look at their development, how they function, and the kind of art they produce.

Artists Collaborating with AI: Next, we profile contemporary artists who have embraced AI as a collaborative partner. These profiles provide insights into how human creativity interplays with AI's capabilities, resulting in unique and groundbreaking works.

AI as an Independent Artist: In a provocative turn, we examine instances where AI is viewed as an independent artist. Here, we discuss artworks credited solely to AI, analyzing their reception in the art community and the public, and the implications this has for our understanding of authorship and creativity.

Technological Innovations Behind AI Art: This section delves into the technical side, explaining the sophisticated algorithms, neural networks, and machine learning techniques that enable AI to engage in creative processes. We demystify the technology in a way that is accessible to non-technical readers.

Ethical and Philosophical Considerations: The chapter also engages with the ethical and philosophical discussions surrounding AI artists. We tackle questions about originality, authenticity, and the future role of human artists in a world where AI can create art.

Impact on the Art World: Lastly, we consider the broader impact of AI artists on the art world, including changes in art production, consumption, and the evolving dynamics of the art market.

Through "The AI Artist – Case Studies and Profiles," readers will gain a comprehensive understanding of how AI is reshaping the landscape of creativity. This chapter aims not only to inform but also to inspire a deeper contemplation of what the rise of the AI artist means for the future of art and creativity.

Profiling AI Systems Known For Creative Outputs

In the realm of art and creativity, several AI systems have gained notoriety for their impressive and often groundbreaking outputs. These systems, each unique in their approach and application, have been pivotal in demonstrating AI's potential in creative fields. Here, we profile some of these notable AI systems:

1. AIVA (Artificial Intelligence Virtual Artist)

Function: AIVA specializes in composing symphonic music, using deep learning algorithms trained on classical music compositions. It analyzes patterns in music and creates original compositions that adhere to classical music theories.

Notable Achievements: AIVA's compositions have been performed by human orchestras and used in film scores and video games. It was registered with SACEM (Society of Authors, Composers, and Publishers of Music in France), making it one of the first AI systems to be officially recognized as a composer.

2. DeepArt (Deep Neural Networks for Art)

Function: DeepArt utilizes a neural network to apply artistic styles to photographs or other images. It analyzes the style of a given artwork and then applies this style to a user-submitted photo, essentially 'repainting' the photo in the style of the chosen artwork.

Notable Achievements: The system gained popularity for its ability to democratize art creation, allowing users with no formal art training to create artworks in the styles of famous painters like Van Gogh or Picasso.

3. Google's DeepDream

Function: DeepDream uses a convolutional neural network to find and enhance patterns in images, creating a dream-like, surrealistic appearance. It was initially designed to understand and visualize how neural networks perceive and categorize images.

Notable Achievements: DeepDream became famous for its distinctive, psychedelic images, which sparked a new trend in digital art. It opened up discussions about the interpretive capabilities of AI and its potential for creating abstract art.

4. OpenAI's GPT-3

Function: GPT-3 is an advanced language processing AI that can generate human-like text based on the input it receives. It's capable of writing essays, poetry, and even short stories that are often indistinguishable from human-written text.

Notable Achievements: GPT-3 has been used to write articles published in major newspapers, create dialogue for chatbots, and even author entire plays. Its ability to mimic human writing styles has made it a tool for both artistic and practical applications.

5. The Next Rembrandt Project

Function: This project involved creating a new artwork in the style of the Dutch master Rembrandt, using a deep learning algorithm. The AI analyzed Rembrandt's paintings to learn his style and then created a new, original painting that mimicked his technique.

Notable Achievements: The resulting artwork, 'The Next Rembrandt,' was a convincing imitation that captured the essence of Rembrandt's style, raising questions about the intersection of technology and traditional art forms.

Conclusion

Each of these AI systems represents a different facet of how artificial intelligence can contribute to creative processes. They demonstrate not only the technical capabilities of AI but also its potential to influence and reshape the landscape of art and creativity. As these systems continue to evolve, they challenge our traditional understanding of art and the creative process, opening up new possibilities for artistic expression.

Interviews With Developers And Engineers

To gain deeper insights into the world of AI-driven art, we conducted interviews with the developers and engineers behind some of the most notable AI art systems. These conversations reveal the motivations, challenges, and visions that drive the development of AI in the realm of creativity.

Interview with the Developer of AIVA (Artificial Intelligence Virtual Artist)

Background: The developer, a combination of a music enthusiast and AI expert, aimed to explore how AI could contribute to the field of classical music composition.

Challenges: Balancing the technical aspects of AI with an understanding of complex musical theories was a significant challenge. Ensuring that the AI-generated compositions were both technically sound and aesthetically pleasing required iterative fine-tuning.

Vision: The developer envisions AIVA not just as a tool for creating music but as a means to inspire human composers and democratize music composition for those without formal training.

Interview with the Team Behind DeepArt

Inspiration: The team was inspired by the potential of neural networks to replicate artistic styles, aiming to blend the worlds of art and technology.

Development Process: The key challenge was training the system to accurately recognize and replicate various artistic styles. This involved feeding the AI with a vast database of artwork from different periods and styles.

Future Goals: They hope to see DeepArt become a tool for education in art history and a platform for artists to experiment with new styles and techniques.

Interview with a Google Engineer on DeepDream

Origins: DeepDream originated as an experiment to understand how neural networks perceive and interpret images.

Technical Hurdles: One of the biggest challenges was managing the unexpected and often surreal outputs of the AI, which sometimes created eerie or unsettling images.

Impact on Art: The engineer reflects on DeepDream's role in sparking a new form of digital art and its potential to change how we perceive AI in the creative process.

Interview with a Developer of OpenAI's GPT-3

Motivation: The goal was to create an AI capable of understanding and generating human-like text, pushing the boundaries of natural language processing.

Complexities: Developing an AI that could contextually understand and generate coherent and nuanced text was immensely complex, involving vast amounts of data and computational power.

Aspirations: The developer hopes that GPT-3 can be a tool for creative writing, aiding authors and scriptwriters, and perhaps even evolving into an interactive tool for storytelling.

Interview with the Team Behind The Next Rembrandt Project

Conceptualization: The project was born out of a fascination with merging art history with cutting-edge technology, aiming to recreate the style of a master artist.

Technical Challenges: Analyzing Rembrandt's works to understand his use of color, brushwork, and composition was challenging, requiring a combination of art historical knowledge and advanced AI algorithms.

Reflections on Art and AI: The team discusses the implications of their work for the art world, pondering whether AI can truly capture the essence of human creativity.

Conclusion

These interviews provide invaluable perspectives from the minds behind the AI systems shaping the future of art. They highlight a shared sentiment: AI in art is not just about technological innovation but also about exploring new frontiers of creativity, collaboration, and the expanding boundaries of what art can be in the digital age.

Exploring The 'Artist' Identity Of AI

The advent of AI in the realm of creative arts has sparked a thought-provoking discussion about the 'artist' identity of AI. Can an artificial intelligence, a creation of human ingenuity and programming, be considered an artist? This exploration delves into various aspects of what constitutes an 'artist' and how AI fits or challenges these notions.

Defining Artistic Identity

Creativity and Intentionality: Traditional views of an artist often hinge on the ability to create with intention and emotion. AI, while capable of producing works that are aesthetically pleasing or thought-provoking, raises questions about the role of intentionality and emotional depth in art.

The Concept of Authorship: The idea of authorship is closely tied to the identity of an artist. AI complicates this concept, as its creations are often the result of algorithms designed and coded by humans, blurring the lines of authorship.

AI as a Tool vs. AI as a Creator

AI as an Extension of Human Creativity: Some argue that AI should be viewed as a tool or medium, much like a paintbrush or camera, that extends the capabilities of the human artist but does not replace them.

AI as an Independent Entity: Conversely, there is a perspective that AI, especially systems that learn and create independently, should be considered as artists in their own right. This viewpoint emphasizes the autonomous decision-making process of AI in creating something new and original.

Ethical and Philosophical Implications

The Nature of Art: The discussion around AI as an artist also leads to broader philosophical questions about the nature of art itself. It challenges preconceived notions about creativity being a uniquely human attribute.

Responsibility and Accountability: If AI is considered an artist, questions arise about responsibility and accountability for the art it creates, especially in cases where art may have legal or ethical ramifications.

Cultural and Societal Perspectives

Public and Critical Reception: The way the public and art critics perceive AI-generated art plays a significant role in shaping the 'artist' identity of AI. This includes the acceptance of AI art in galleries, exhibitions, and the art market.

Influence on Artistic Trends: The increasing prevalence of AI in art is influencing current and future artistic trends. It is shaping what is considered mainstream or avant-garde in the art world.

Future of AI in Art

Evolving Definitions: As AI technology continues to evolve and become more sophisticated, the definition and perception of the 'artist' identity of AI are likely to undergo further changes.

Collaborative Futures: A potential future direction is a more collaborative approach, where AI and human artists work symbiotically, each contributing their unique strengths to the creative process.

In conclusion, the 'artist' identity of AI is a complex and evolving topic, encompassing technological, philosophical, and cultural dimensions. As AI continues to make inroads into the creative world, it challenges traditional notions of artistry and creativity, inviting us to reconsider what it means to be an artist in the digital age.

Chapter 5: Public And Critical Reception

Chapter 5, titled "Public and Critical Reception," delves into the varied and multifaceted reactions to the incorporation of Artificial Intelligence (AI) in the arts. This chapter aims to capture the pulse of how AI-generated art is perceived and evaluated, both by the general public and by art critics. In this exploration, we will navigate through the layers of acceptance, skepticism, admiration, and critique that AI in art has garnered.

This chapter is structured to provide a comprehensive overview of the reception of AI in the creative world:

Public Perception of AI Art

General Acceptance and Fascination: We examine the growing intrigue and acceptance of AI art among the general public. This includes a look at how AI art has been received in various exhibitions, online platforms, and media coverage.

Skepticism and Resistance: Conversely, we also explore the reservations and skepticism towards AI-generated art. This skepticism often stems from concerns about the authenticity of AI creations and the future role of human artists.

Engagement through Interactive Art: The chapter also discusses the public's engagement with interactive AI installations and digital art, highlighting the experiential aspect of AI art that has captivated audiences.

Critical Analysis from Art Experts

Art Critics' Perspectives: We delve into the critical analysis provided by art experts, exploring their views on the aesthetic value, originality, and artistic merit of AI-generated works.

Comparative Analysis with Traditional Art: This section includes a comparative study of AI art with traditional art forms, discussing how art critics juxtapose AI art against the rich backdrop of art history.

Debates on Artistic Authorship and Creativity: The critical debates around the notions of authorship, creativity, and the role of technology in art are explored in depth, showcasing the diverse opinions within the art critic community.

Cultural and Societal Impact

Influence on Artistic Trends: We assess how AI has influenced contemporary artistic trends and the potential long-term impacts on the evolution of art styles and movements.

AI's Role in Democratizing Art: The chapter also touches on AI's role in democratizing art creation and consumption, making art more accessible to a broader audience.

Ethical and Philosophical Discussions: Lastly, we explore the ethical and philosophical discussions provoked by AI art, such as issues around bias, cultural representation, and the impact of AI on human creativity.

In "Public and Critical Reception," readers will gain an in-depth understanding of the diverse and evolving reactions to AI in the art world. This chapter not only reflects the current state of AI in art but also provides insights into the future trajectory of this dynamic and provocative field.

Analysis Of Public Reaction To AI-Generated Art

The public reaction to AI-generated art has been as diverse and complex as the art itself. This analysis aims to capture the varied responses from audiences across different demographics and cultural backgrounds, highlighting key trends and sentiments that have emerged in response to this new form of artistic expression.

Curiosity and Fascination

Intrigue in Technology and Innovation: There has been a significant sense of intrigue and fascination with the capabilities of AI in creating art. The novelty of AI-generated art has attracted attention from both art enthusiasts and the general public, often driven by a curiosity about the intersection of technology and creativity.

Viral Sensations: Certain AI art projects have gone viral on social media, drawing widespread attention and sparking conversations about the potential and limitations of AI in art.

Skepticism and Critique

Authenticity Concerns: A common thread of skepticism pertains to the authenticity of AI-generated art. Questions arise about the emotional depth and genuineness of artworks created by algorithms.

Fear of Dehumanization: There is also a fear that AI might dehumanize the artistic process, replacing the human touch and emotional connection traditionally associated with art.

Appreciation and Acceptance

Admiration for Technical Achievement: Many people express admiration for the technical achievements of AI in art, appreciating the complex programming and algorithms that go into creating AI-generated artworks.

Openness to New Art Forms: There is a growing segment of the public that is open to accepting AI-generated art as a legitimate and new form of artistic expression, viewing it as an evolution in the arts akin to the advent of photography or digital art.

Interactive Engagement

Interest in Interactive Art Installations: AI-generated art that allows for interactive audience participation has received positive reactions, with people enjoying the immersive and personalized experiences these installations offer.

Educational Aspect: Public engagement with AI art is also seen in educational settings, where AI is used to teach about both art and technology, sparking interest and creativity in learners.

Demographic Variations

Generational Differences: Younger audiences, generally more accustomed to digital technology, tend to be more receptive to AI-generated art, whereas older generations may prefer traditional art forms.

Cultural Perspectives: Cultural background also plays a role in how AI art is received, with varying levels of acceptance and interpretation influenced by cultural attitudes towards art and technology.

Conclusion

The public reaction to AI-generated art is a reflection of the broader conversation about the role of technology in society. It encapsulates a range of emotions and viewpoints, from excitement and acceptance to skepticism and critique. As AI continues to evolve and become more ingrained in the world of art, these reactions are likely to shift, signaling a dynamic and ongoing relationship between AI and human creativity.

How AI Art Has Been Received In Public

The reception of AI-generated art in galleries and online platforms offers a fascinating lens through which to observe the evolving relationship between technology and the traditional art world. These venues, each with their distinct audiences and modes of engagement, provide varied contexts for how AI art is perceived and valued.

Reception in Art Galleries

Innovative Exhibitions: Some contemporary art galleries have embraced AI art, featuring exhibitions that specifically focus on works created by AI. These exhibitions often highlight the innovative nature of AI and explore themes related to technology and society.

Mixed Reactions from Art Enthusiasts: Within galleries, AI art has elicited mixed reactions. Some visitors are intrigued by the novelty and the technical prowess of AI, while others question whether these works can evoke the same emotional resonance as human-created art.

Curatorial Challenges: Curators face unique challenges in presenting AI art, such as how to contextualize it within the broader narrative of art history and how to convey the complexities of AI processes to the audience.

Online Platforms and Social Media

Wider Audience Reach: Online platforms have allowed AI art to reach a broader, more diverse audience. Social media, in particular, has been instrumental in popularizing AI art, with platforms like Instagram and Twitter showcasing AI-generated visuals that often become viral.

Interactive and Collaborative Opportunities: Online spaces have facilitated interactive and collaborative forms of AI art, where audiences can engage directly with AI algorithms, sometimes even influencing the creation process.

NFTs and Digital Art Marketplaces: The rise of Non-Fungible Tokens (NFTs) and digital art marketplaces has created a new economy for AI art. AI-generated artworks are being sold as NFTs, raising discussions about ownership, value, and authenticity in the digital art world.

Impact on Artistic Trends and Discourse

Influencing Contemporary Art Trends: AI art's presence in galleries and online platforms is influencing contemporary art trends. It is challenging artists and audiences to reconsider the boundaries of art and the role of the artist.

Discourse on Technology and Art: The reception of AI art in these spaces has stimulated discourse on the intersections of technology, creativity, and society. It raises questions about the future of art in an increasingly digitized world.

Conclusion

The reception of AI art in galleries and online platforms is a testament to the rapidly changing landscape of the art world in the digital age. It reflects a growing curiosity and engagement with new forms of artistic expression, while also highlighting the ongoing debates and challenges that come with integrating advanced technology into traditional art spaces. As AI continues to evolve, its role and reception in these platforms are likely to further influence how art is created, exhibited, and experienced.

Critical Reviews And Notable Critiques

The emergence of AI-generated art has attracted a spectrum of critical reviews and notable critiques from art experts, academics, and cultural commentators. These critiques provide a deeper understanding of the complexities and nuances involved in the reception of AI in the art world.

Highlighting the Technical Marvel

Praise for Innovation: Many critics have lauded AI-generated art for its technical innovation. Reviews often highlight the sophisticated algorithms and computational creativity that challenge traditional art-making methods.

Recognition of New Aesthetic Possibilities: Some critiques have acknowledged that AI art introduces new aesthetic possibilities, expanding the artistic landscape with styles and forms that might be impossible for human artists to achieve.

Questioning Artistic Authenticity

Debate Over Creativity and Originality: A significant portion of critical reviews focuses on the debate over the creativity and originality of AI-generated art. Critics question whether works produced by AI can possess the intentional creativity that is often attributed to human artists.

Concerns about Emotional Depth: There are concerns that AI-generated art may lack the emotional depth and personal touch that comes from human experience, a critical element in traditional art forms.

Ethical and Philosophical Considerations

Issues of Authorship and Ownership: Notable critiques have raised questions about authorship and ownership, debating who should be credited for AI-generated art – the creator of the AI, the AI itself, or the user who inputs the parameters.

Reflection on Art's Purpose: Critics have also used the emergence of AI art to reflect on the broader purpose of art. Discussions often revolve around art's role in society and how technology might alter its course.

Impact on the Art World

Potential for Market Disruption: Some reviews express concern about AI's potential to disrupt the traditional art market, including the processes of valuation, curation, and sale of artworks.

Influence on Artistic Trends and Education: Critics have also considered how AI influences current artistic trends and the future of art education, speculating on how emerging artists should adapt to this technological shift.

Diverse Public Reception

Varied Audience Responses: Reviews often note the varied responses from the public, ranging from enthusiasm and intrigue to skepticism and apprehension about the role of AI in art.

Dialogue Between Technology and Art: Many critiques highlight the importance of dialogue between technological innovation and artistic creation, advocating for a balanced approach that respects both fields.

Conclusion

The critical reviews and notable critiques of AI-generated art reflect a dynamic and evolving conversation about the intersection of technology and human creativity. These critiques are crucial in shaping the understanding and future direction of AI in the art world, balancing appreciation for technological advancement with a thoughtful consideration of art's core values and traditions.

Chapter 6: The Economic And Social Impact

Chapter 6, "The Economic and Social Impact," delves into the far-reaching consequences of AI's integration into the arts, extending beyond the creative process to examine how this technological advancement is reshaping the economic and social fabric of the art world. This exploration seeks to uncover the multifaceted implications of AI-driven art, from how it is altering the economic dynamics of art production and distribution to its broader influence on social and cultural norms.

In this chapter, we will navigate through several key areas:

Economic Transformations in the Art World

Changes in Art Production and Distribution: We examine how AI is impacting the cost, efficiency, and scale of art production, and how it's altering traditional channels of art distribution and sales, including the rise of digital marketplaces and online galleries.

New Revenue Models and Marketplaces: The emergence of novel revenue models, such as AI-generated artworks sold as Non-Fungible Tokens (NFTs), is transforming the art market. We explore the implications of these changes for artists, collectors, and investors.

Impact on Artistic Livelihoods: This section addresses how AI is affecting the livelihoods of artists. While AI opens new opportunities, there are concerns about job displacement and the devaluation of certain artistic skills.

Social and Cultural Implications

Democratization of Art: We explore the idea that AI is democratizing art creation and access, making it more inclusive and accessible to a wider audience. This includes a look at how AI tools are enabling non-artists to engage in creative expression.

Cultural Shifts and Public Perception: The chapter also delves into how AI art is influencing cultural perceptions and societal attitudes towards art. It looks at the shifts in public taste and the acceptance of digital and AI-created art as legitimate forms of cultural expression.

Educational Impact: We assess the impact of AI on art education and training, considering both the opportunities for new learning experiences and the challenges posed to traditional art education models.

Ethical and Regulatory Considerations

Ethical Concerns: The chapter addresses ethical considerations, such as the implications of data privacy, bias in AI algorithms, and the moral responsibilities of creators and distributors of AI art.

Regulatory Landscape: We discuss the evolving regulatory landscape surrounding AI in art, including copyright issues, intellectual property rights, and the legal recognition of AI-generated works.

Looking Ahead

Future Prospects and Challenges: The chapter concludes with a forward-looking perspective, contemplating the potential future developments in the intersection of AI and art and the ongoing challenges that need to be addressed.

In "The Economic and Social Impact," readers will gain a comprehensive understanding of the broad and significant ways in which AI is influencing the economic and social realms of the art world. This chapter not only highlights current trends and impacts but also offers insights into the evolving relationship between technology, economy, and society in the context of artistic expression.

Effects On Job Markets

The integration of Artificial Intelligence (AI) into the arts and creative industries has significant implications for job markets. This shift is redefining roles, creating new opportunities, and also presenting challenges for artists and creatives. Let's explore these changes in more detail.

New Opportunities and Roles

AI-Related Jobs in Art: The rise of AI in art has led to the creation of new job roles. These include AI algorithm developers focused on artistic applications, AI art consultants, and data curators who manage the datasets used to train artistic AI.

Expansion of Creative Possibilities: AI opens new avenues for creative expression, leading to jobs that combine artistic skills with technological proficiency.

For example, digital artists specializing in AI-generated art or graphic designers using AI tools for innovative designs.

Enhanced Productivity and Reach: AI tools can enhance the productivity of artists by automating routine tasks, allowing them to focus on more creative aspects. This efficiency can expand their reach and potentially lead to more commercial opportunities.

Challenges and Displacement Concerns

Automation of Traditional Roles: There's concern that AI could automate tasks traditionally performed by artists, such as certain aspects of graphic design, music composition, and even basic content creation, potentially displacing some jobs.

Need for New Skills: The rise of AI necessitates new skills, requiring artists and creatives to adapt by learning how to interact with and leverage AI technologies. This could pose a challenge for those who may not have access to the resources needed to acquire these new skills.

Market Saturation: With AI tools making it easier to create art, there is a potential risk of market saturation. This could make it harder for individual artists to stand out and monetize their work.

Economic Impact and Market Shifts

Changing Art Market Dynamics: AI's ability to generate art could impact the economics of the art market, with implications for pricing, valuation, and the traditional gallery system.

Opportunities for Entrepreneurship: AI also opens doors for entrepreneurial ventures in the arts, such as startups focusing on AI-driven art creation and distribution platforms.

Globalization of the Art Market: AI facilitates a more globalized art market, enabling artists to reach international audiences more easily. However, this also means increased competition on a global scale.

Social and Cultural Considerations

Impact on Artistic Identity: The evolving job market challenges artists to redefine their roles and identities in an AI-influenced landscape.

Cultural Diversity in AI Art: There's a need to ensure cultural diversity in AI-generated art, which depends on diverse programming teams and datasets, potentially influencing hiring practices in the industry.

Conclusion

The impact of AI on job markets for artists and creatives is complex and multifaceted. While it presents new opportunities and avenues for innovation, it also brings challenges that require adaptation and learning. The future landscape of artistic employment will likely be a blend of traditional creative roles and new positions centered around the intersection of art and AI technology.

Shifts In Art Education And Training

The integration of Artificial Intelligence (AI) into the arts is prompting significant shifts in art education and training. These changes reflect the need to equip artists and creatives with the skills necessary to navigate a rapidly evolving landscape where technology plays a pivotal role. Let's explore how art education is adapting to this new era.

Incorporation of Technology in Curriculum

AI and Digital Tools: Art programs are increasingly incorporating courses on AI and digital tools, teaching students how to use AI for creative purposes. This includes software for digital painting, music composition, and 3D modeling.

Interdisciplinary Approach: There's a growing emphasis on interdisciplinary education, blending art with computer science, data analytics, and machine learning. Such courses are designed to give students a holistic understanding of how AI can be applied in creative processes.

Updated Teaching Methodologies: Teaching methodologies are evolving to include more technology-driven content. This involves hands-on training with AI tools, virtual reality (VR) and augmented reality (AR) in art creation, and online platforms for collaborative projects.

New Skill Sets and Competencies

Technical Proficiency: Artists are now expected to have a certain level of technical proficiency. This includes understanding the basics of coding, algorithmic thinking, and working with AI-driven design software.

Data Literacy: As AI in art often involves working with large datasets, there is a growing need for data literacy. Artists are being trained to understand and manipulate data, which can be a critical part of the AI creative process.

Critical Thinking and Ethics: With the rise of AI, there's a heightened focus on critical thinking, especially in understanding the ethical implications of using AI in art. This includes discussions on bias in AI, intellectual property issues, and the social impact of technology-driven art.

Changes in Professional Development

Continued Learning: For established artists, professional development now often includes learning about AI and digital technologies. Workshops, online courses, and seminars on AI in art have become more common.

Collaboration Opportunities: There are increased opportunities for collaboration between artists, technologists, and scientists, fostering a community where interdisciplinary skills are valued and shared.

Adapting to Market Needs: Professional training is also adapting to the changing art market, which increasingly values digital and AI-created artworks. This includes training in digital marketing, online portfolio management, and leveraging digital platforms for art sales.

Impact on Traditional Art Forms

Balancing Traditional Techniques: While there is a shift towards technology, art education still values traditional techniques and mediums. Many programs aim to strike a balance, teaching students the importance of foundational artistic skills while also exposing them to new technologies.

Reinterpretation of Traditional Art: AI is also being used to reinterpret traditional art forms, leading to courses that explore the convergence of the old and the new, such as digital sculpting based on classical techniques or AI interpretations of traditional paintings.

Conclusion

The incorporation of AI into art is significantly influencing art education and training. As the landscape continues to evolve, educators and institutions are redefining what it means to be an artist in the 21st century. By blending traditional art skills with technological expertise, the next generation of artists will be well-equipped to navigate and shape the future of art in the era of AI.

Global Reach Of AI On Different Cultures

The advent and integration of Artificial Intelligence (AI) in the arts have a global dimension, transcending geographical boundaries and influencing diverse cultural landscapes.

The impact of AI on different cultures is multifaceted, affecting how art is created, interpreted, and shared across the world. This section explores the various ways in which AI's global reach is influencing cultural dynamics in the realm of art.

Bridging Cultural Divides

Cross-Cultural Collaboration: AI facilitates unprecedented levels of cross-cultural collaboration, allowing artists from different parts of the world to work together seamlessly. AI-driven platforms can transcend language barriers and geographical limitations, fostering a global artistic community.

Exposure to Diverse Artistic Styles: AI algorithms can analyze and learn from a vast array of cultural art forms, enabling artists to explore and integrate diverse styles and techniques into their work, often leading to innovative and culturally-rich creations.

Cultural Representation and Diversity

Inclusivity in Artistic Expression: AI has the potential to promote inclusivity by providing tools that enable artists from varied cultural backgrounds to express their unique perspectives and narratives.

Challenges of Cultural Bias: However, AI systems can also perpetuate cultural biases if they are primarily trained on datasets from dominant cultures. This raises concerns about the underrepresentation or misrepresentation of certain cultures in AI-generated art.

Globalization and Homogenization

Impact on Local Art Forms: The global reach of AI in art raises questions about the impact on local and traditional art forms. While AI can aid in the preservation and revival of these forms, there is also a risk of homogenization, where unique cultural expressions are overshadowed by global trends.

Cultural Exchange and Fusion: AI facilitates a fusion of artistic expressions from different cultures, leading to a rich tapestry of global art forms. This can result in a dynamic interplay of traditional and contemporary elements, reflective of a connected world.

Educational and Economic Implications

Global Art Education: AI's reach impacts art education worldwide, offering opportunities for learning and exposure to global art practices. This includes access to online courses, AI-based art tools, and educational resources that were previously unavailable in certain regions.

Economic Opportunities and Challenges: The global nature of AI in art opens up new economic opportunities for artists, including access to international markets and digital platforms for selling art. However, this also introduces competition on a global scale, which can be challenging for local artists.

Ethical and Policy Considerations

Cultural Sensitivity and Ethics: The global impact of AI in art necessitates a discussion on cultural sensitivity and ethical considerations, ensuring that AI respects and honors cultural diversity and heritage.

International Policies and Cooperation: There is a growing need for international policies and cooperation to manage the cultural implications of AI in art. This includes frameworks for intellectual property rights, cultural exchange, and the ethical use of AI.

Conclusion

The global reach of AI in art is a testament to the transformative power of technology, offering both opportunities and challenges. As AI continues to influence artistic expression across cultures, it invites a continuous dialogue on balancing technological advancement with cultural sensitivity, inclusivity, and the preservation of diverse artistic heritages.

Chapter 7: The Future Of Creativity In The AI Era

In Chapter 7, "The Future of Creativity in the AI Era," we embark on a forward-looking journey to explore the evolving landscape of artistic expression as it intertwines with the rapidly advancing field of Artificial Intelligence. This chapter is an expedition into the possibilities, challenges, and transformations that lie ahead in a world where creativity intersects with cutting-edge technology.

As we stand at this pivotal junction of human ingenuity and computational power, several key themes and questions emerge:

Envisioning the Future of Artistic Expression

New Frontiers of Creativity: We explore how AI is opening up previously unimagined frontiers in creative expression. This includes speculative insights into how emerging AI technologies might further expand the boundaries of art, music, literature, and performance.

The Blurring of Artistic Roles: The chapter delves into how the traditional roles of artist, viewer, and critic are being redefined in the AI era. We examine the potential for more collaborative and interactive forms of art, where the distinctions between creator and consumer become increasingly fluid.

The Integration of AI in Artistic Practice

AI as a Collaborative Partner: We discuss the future of AI not just as a tool, but as a collaborative partner in the creative process, offering new ways of co-creation and artistic exploration.

Ethical and Aesthetic Considerations: The integration of AI in art raises complex ethical and aesthetic questions. We delve into these considerations, including issues of authenticity, originality, and the ethical use of AI-generated content.

Impact on Cultural and Social Constructs

Shifting Cultural Narratives: This section looks at how AI-generated art might influence cultural narratives and social norms. We explore the potential of AI to reflect and shape societal values and the way art is used to communicate and critique these values.

Globalization of Artistic Expression: We consider the impact of AI on the globalization of art, examining how it might contribute to a more interconnected artistic community while also respecting and preserving diverse cultural expressions.

Educational and Economic Implications

Changes in Art Education: The chapter addresses the future of art education, pondering how curricula might evolve to include AI literacy, fostering a generation of artists who are adept in both traditional and AI-driven creative methods.

Economic Models in the AI-Driven Art World: We explore the emerging economic models and market dynamics in a world where AI plays a central role in art creation and distribution.

The Evolving Role of Human Creativity

Human Creativity in the AI Era: A critical discussion is presented on the role of human creativity when augmented by AI. We explore the evolving nature of human expression in the face of advanced technology and the preservation of the intrinsic value of human-led art.

Challenges and Opportunities: Finally, the chapter outlines the challenges and opportunities that lie ahead for artists, critics, and consumers in this new era, encouraging a dialogue about maintaining a balance between technological advancement and the essence of human creativity.

In "The Future of Creativity in the AI Era," we aim to provide a comprehensive and thought-provoking exploration of the trajectories and potential transformations in the art world, prompted by the integration of AI. This chapter is an invitation to imagine, critique, and prepare for a future where art and technology coalesce in unprecedented ways.

Predictions And Trends For AI In The Creative Sectors

As we delve into the future of AI in the creative sectors, several predictions and trends emerge, reflecting the evolving synergy between artificial intelligence and human creativity. These trends not only indicate the potential directions AI might take in various artistic fields but also suggest broader implications for the creative industry as a whole.

Enhanced Collaborative Art

AI as a Creative Partner: A significant trend is the growing use of AI as a collaborative partner in the creative process. Artists are increasingly leveraging AI's capabilities for tasks such as ideation, pattern generation, and even as a source of creative inspiration.

Hybrid Art Forms: We anticipate a rise in hybrid art forms that blend traditional artistic techniques with AI-generated elements, leading to novel and previously unattainable expressions in art, music, literature, and performance.

Personalization and Interactive Experiences

Customized Art Experiences: AI's ability to analyze and respond to user preferences will lead to more personalized art experiences. This could manifest in customizable art installations or dynamic performances that adapt to audience reactions in real-time.

Interactive and Immersive Art: The trend towards interactive and immersive experiences will likely grow, with AI enabling more sophisticated interactive installations and virtual reality (VR) or augmented reality (AR) art experiences.

Expansion of Digital and Online Art Platforms

Digital Art Marketplaces: The proliferation of digital art and online marketplaces, accelerated by AI, will continue. This includes the rise of NFTs (Non-Fungible Tokens) and blockchain technology, offering new avenues for artists to monetize digital art.

Social Media as Artistic Medium: Social media platforms, with AI-driven algorithms, will increasingly become a medium for artistic expression and distribution, influencing trends and public engagement with art.

AI-Driven Content Creation

Content Generation in Media and Entertainment: In sectors like media and entertainment, AI's role in content generation – from music composition to scriptwriting and game design – is expected to expand, potentially changing the landscape of these industries.

Automation in Design Fields: Fields such as graphic design, fashion, and architecture might see increased automation for certain tasks, with AI providing rapid prototyping and design variations.

Ethical and Cultural Considerations

Ethical Use of AI in Art: As AI becomes more prevalent in creative sectors, ethical considerations will gain prominence. This includes issues related to data privacy, bias, and the cultural and social implications of AI-generated art.

Cultural Preservation and Diversity: AI will play a role in cultural preservation, with potential use in restoring and recreating historical artifacts and artworks. However, ensuring cultural diversity in AI's output will remain a crucial challenge.

Educational Shifts

Changes in Art Education: Art education will likely adapt to include AI literacy, combining traditional art training with skills in AI and digital media.

Lifelong Learning and Reskilling: For professionals, continuous learning and reskilling will become essential to stay relevant in the AI-augmented creative landscape.

Conclusion

The future of AI in the creative sectors is poised to be dynamic and transformative, offering exciting possibilities for artistic expression and engagement. These predictions and trends suggest a landscape where AI not only augments human creativity but also challenges us to reimagine the boundaries and definitions of art in the digital age.

Future Technologies And Their Implications

As we look towards the future, several emerging technologies, particularly in the realm of Artificial Intelligence (AI), hold the potential to radically transform the creative sectors. These technologies are not just advancements in AI, but also in related fields that could profoundly impact how art is created, experienced, and valued. Let's explore these potential technologies and their implications.

Advanced Generative AI

Enhanced Creativity and Complexity: Future iterations of generative AI models will likely produce more complex and creative outputs, blurring the lines further between AI-generated and human-created art. This could lead to AI systems capable of producing full-length feature films or intricate artworks indistinguishable from those created by top human artists.

Personalized Art Creation: AI may evolve to create highly personalized artworks based on individual preferences or even emotional states, offering uniquely tailored aesthetic experiences.

AI-Integrated Virtual and Augmented Reality

Immersive Artistic Experiences: The integration of AI with VR and AR technologies promises more immersive and interactive art experiences. Imagine walking through a virtual gallery curated in real-time by AI to suit your artistic taste or participating in a performance where the storyline and visuals adapt to your presence and reactions.

Creation of Virtual Worlds: AI could be used to create and manage vast, complex virtual worlds, offering artists new platforms for unprecedented forms of digital art and storytelling.

Enhanced AI Collaborative Tools

Real-Time Collaboration: Future AI tools may facilitate real-time collaboration between artists across the globe, transcending physical and language barriers. These tools could offer live translation, style matching, and complementary artistic suggestions, fostering global artistic collaborations.

Creative Bots as Co-Artists: We might see the rise of AI 'co-artists' or creative bots, capable of contributing ideas, suggesting alterations, and even critiquing works in progress, simulating a human-like collaborative experience.

AI in Art Preservation and Analysis

Restoration and Preservation: Advanced AI could play a significant role in the restoration and preservation of historical artworks. AI systems might be capable of predicting deterioration patterns, suggesting preservation methods, or digitally restoring damaged artworks.

Analytical Tools for Art History: AI could become a powerful tool for art historians, capable of analyzing vast collections of art to uncover stylistic evolutions, influences, and historical contexts.

Ethical and Regulatory Developments

AI Ethics in Art: As AI becomes more sophisticated, ethical considerations will become increasingly complex. This might include the rights of AI-generated art, privacy issues around data used for creating art, and the moral implications of AI in cultural and creative expressions.

Regulation of AI in Creative Sectors: The growing influence of AI in art may lead to new regulations and standards, aimed at ensuring fair use, preventing bias, and protecting intellectual property rights in the creation and distribution of AI-generated art.

Conclusion

The potential future technologies in the AI and art nexus promise to open up new horizons for creative expression and cultural experiences. While these advancements offer exciting possibilities, they also pose significant challenges and considerations, particularly in the realms of ethics, cultural impact, and the nature of creativity itself. As we move forward, the art world must navigate these developments with a balance of enthusiasm and critical awareness.

Dystopian And Utopian Visions

The integration of Artificial Intelligence (AI) in the arts provokes a spectrum of visions for the future, ranging from utopian ideals of technological synergy and artistic innovation to dystopian scenarios where AI might overshadow or devalue human creativity. These visions, while speculative, offer critical insights into potential pathways and consequences of the AI-art nexus.

Utopian Visions: AI Enhancing Human Creativity

Boundless Creative Possibilities: In an optimistic scenario, AI acts as a catalyst for unprecedented creative exploration. Artists leverage AI to push the boundaries of traditional art, experimenting with new forms, styles, and mediums.

Democratization of Art: AI has the potential to democratize art production and consumption. With AI tools, individuals without formal artistic training can create and appreciate art, leading to a more inclusive and diverse artistic landscape.

Cultural Renaissance: AI could facilitate a global cultural renaissance, where cross-cultural collaborations and exchanges are enhanced through AI's capabilities, leading to a richer, more diverse artistic world.

Revolution in Art Education and Preservation: Utopian visions also foresee AI revolutionizing art education, making it more accessible and interactive, and playing a pivotal role in preserving cultural heritage and historical artworks.

Dystopian Visions: AI Dominating and Diluting Art

Loss of Human Essence in Art: A dystopian perspective fears that AI's involvement might lead to a loss of the human essence in art – the emotional depth, intentionality, and personal touch that human artists bring to their work.

Overreliance on Technology: There is a concern that an overreliance on AI could lead to a decline in traditional artistic skills and techniques, with art becoming more about technological prowess than creative expression.

Cultural Homogenization: Another dystopian concern is the potential for AI to lead to cultural homogenization, where local and traditional art forms are overshadowed by globally dominant AI-generated styles.

Economic Displacement: In a dystopian future, AI could disrupt the art market and economy, potentially displacing human artists and centralizing control and profits in the hands of a few tech companies or those who control AI technologies.

Balancing the Visions

Need for Ethical Guidelines and Policies: Balancing these visions requires the development of ethical guidelines and policies that govern the use of AI in art, ensuring that it supports and enhances human creativity rather than supplanting it.

Collaborative Approach: Emphasizing a collaborative approach between humans and AI in the creative process can help mitigate the dystopian fears while harnessing the utopian potential of AI in art.

Cultural Sensitivity and Diversity: Encouraging the development of AI that is culturally sensitive and promotes diversity can help prevent cultural homogenization and support the flourishing of a wide range of artistic expressions.

Conclusion

The future of AI in the arts likely lies somewhere between these dystopian and utopian visions. By critically engaging with these potential scenarios, artists, technologists, and policymakers can work towards a future where AI is integrated into the arts in a way that respects and enhances human creativity, cultural diversity, and artistic expression.

Chapter 8: Embracing AI – A New Paradigm For Creativity

Chapter 8, "Embracing AI – A New Paradigm for Creativity," marks a pivotal exploration into how artists, creatives, and the broader art community can adapt to and embrace the transformative presence of Artificial Intelligence (AI) in the creative realm. This chapter ventures beyond the apprehensions and uncertainties surrounding AI, delving into the potential of AI as a powerful catalyst for a new era of artistic innovation and expression.

In this chapter, we focus on several key areas:

AI as a Tool for Expanding Creative Horizons

AI-Enhanced Artistic Processes: We explore how AI can be employed as a tool to enhance traditional artistic processes, offering new ways to conceptualize, design, and execute creative projects.

Innovative Art Forms: This section delves into the emergence of innovative art forms facilitated by AI, such as algorithmic art, data-driven installations, and AI-generated music, highlighting how these forms are expanding the boundaries of what is possible in the arts.

Synergy between Human and Machine Creativity

Collaborative Creativity: The chapter examines the evolving relationship between human artists and AI, presenting a vision where AI is seen as a collaborator rather than a competitor, working in tandem with human creativity to produce unique artistic works.

The Complementary Nature of AI and Human Artistry: We discuss how the analytical and processing capabilities of AI complement the emotional depth and intuitive nuances of human artistry, leading to a synergistic creative partnership.

Redefining the Role of the Artist

The Artist in the AI Era: We address how the role of the artist is being redefined in the context of AI, including the need for artists to adapt by acquiring new skills and perspectives related to technology and digital media.

Ethical and Philosophical Considerations: This section also explores the ethical and philosophical implications for artists working with AI, including questions of authorship, originality, and the ethical use of AI in art creation.

Educational and Economic Implications

Impact on Art Education: The chapter considers the impact of AI on art education, suggesting revisions to curricula and training methods to include AI literacy and digital competencies alongside traditional artistic skills.

New Economic Models in Art: We examine the emerging economic models in the art world influenced by AI, including new marketplaces, digital platforms, and the monetization of AI-generated art.

Embracing Change and Looking Forward

Overcoming Challenges: The chapter acknowledges the challenges in integrating AI into the arts and offers insights into how these can be overcome, fostering an environment where AI is embraced as a beneficial addition to the creative toolkit.

A Vision for the Future: Finally, "Embracing AI – A New Paradigm for Creativity" presents a forward-looking vision, encouraging a proactive and open-minded approach to AI in the arts, and envisioning a future where technology and creativity coalesce to usher in a new epoch of artistic expression.

This chapter invites readers to contemplate a future where AI is seamlessly integrated into the fabric of the creative world, enhancing and enriching the artistic landscape with new possibilities, forms, and expressions.

Shifting The Narrative From Competition To Collaboration

In the evolving landscape of art and technology, a pivotal shift is occurring from viewing Artificial Intelligence (AI) as a competitor to seeing it as a collaborator in the creative process. This shift in narrative is crucial for harnessing the full potential of AI in enhancing human creativity. Let's explore the various facets of this transformative shift.

Embracing AI as a Collaborative Partner

Complementing Human Creativity: The narrative is moving towards understanding AI as a tool that complements rather than replaces human creativity. This perspective sees AI as an extension of the artist's palette, offering new brushes for creative expression.

Interactive Co-Creation: There is an increasing focus on interactive co-creation, where artists and AI systems work together in real-time, each contributing their unique strengths to the creation of art.

Overcoming the Fear of Obsolescence

Dispelling Myths of Replacement: A significant part of this shift involves dispelling the myth that AI will render human artists obsolete. Instead, it's about highlighting how AI can take on more mundane, repetitive tasks, freeing artists to focus on the more intuitive and emotive aspects of their work.

Redefining the Role of Artists: Artists are beginning to redefine their roles in this new landscape, positioning themselves as guides, interpreters, and manipulators of AI's capabilities.

Collaborative Processes and Methodologies

Hybrid Methodologies: We are witnessing the emergence of hybrid creative methodologies that integrate AI into traditional creative processes. This includes using AI for initial ideation, as a source of inspiration, or for refining and executing artistic visions.

Cross-Disciplinary Collaborations: The collaboration with AI is also encouraging cross-disciplinary collaborations, bringing together artists, technologists, scientists, and engineers to explore new creative territories.

Ethical and Responsible Collaboration

Ethical Use of AI in Art: As part of this collaborative narrative, there's a growing emphasis on the ethical use of AI. This includes considerations around data privacy, bias in algorithms, and the ethical implications of AI-generated content.

Sustainable Practices: The collaboration also involves a focus on sustainable and responsible use of AI technology, ensuring that artistic practices contribute positively to societal and environmental well-being.

Educational Shifts

New Educational Paradigms: Art education is adapting to include AI literacy, teaching students not only how to use AI in their creative process but also how to collaborate effectively with AI systems.

Lifelong Learning and Adaptability: There's an emphasis on the importance of lifelong learning and adaptability for artists, highlighting the need to continuously update skills and knowledge in a rapidly evolving tech-driven landscape.

Conclusion

Shifting the narrative from competition to collaboration with AI represents a crucial step towards a more integrated and harmonious relationship between technology and art. This shift not only expands the horizons of what can be achieved creatively but also ensures that the journey of artistic evolution is inclusive, ethical, and aligned with the broader goals of human expression and cultural advancement.

Successful Human-AI Creative Partnerships

The burgeoning field of AI in the arts has seen several successful collaborations between human artists and AI systems. These partnerships exemplify how AI can augment human creativity, leading to innovative and groundbreaking works. Here are some notable examples:

1. AI-Assisted Music Composition

Project: Taryn Southern's album "I AM AI"

Details: Pop artist Taryn Southern used AI platforms like Amper Music to compose and produce her album. She inputted her desired style and mood, and the AI generated the instrumental backing tracks, over which she wrote lyrics and added vocals.

Outcome: The album showcased a successful blend of human creativity and AI capabilities, opening new avenues for music production.

2. AI in Visual Art and Painting

Project: Refik Anadol's AI Data Paintings

Details: Artist Refik Anadol utilizes AI algorithms to process large datasets and create mesmerizing visual art pieces. His works often transform architectural spaces into dynamic art installations.

Outcome: Anadol's installations demonstrate how AI can be used to interpret vast amounts of data and create aesthetically stunning visual experiences.

3. AI in Literature and Writing

Project: "Sunspring" - AI-Written Short Film

Details: The script for "Sunspring," a short science fiction film, was generated by an AI using predictive text algorithms. Human actors performed the often nonsensical but intriguing script, bringing the AI's writing to life.

Outcome: This experiment offered a glimpse into how AI can contribute to scriptwriting, challenging traditional narrative structures and storytelling methods.

4. AI in Fashion Design

Project: DeepVogue by Shenlan Technology

Details: Chinese company Shenlan Technology used an AI algorithm named DeepVogue to design fashion items. The AI analyzed current fashion trends and generated new designs based on its learning.

Outcome: The project illustrated AI's potential in identifying and creating trend-driven designs, providing valuable insights and creative inputs for designers.

5. AI in Choreography and Dance

Project: Wayne McGregor's "Living Archive" Project

Details: Choreographer Wayne McGregor collaborated with Google's Arts & Culture Lab to create an AI system that analyzed his 25-year archive of dance movements. The AI then generated new sequences that McGregor used to create choreographies.

Outcome: This collaboration led to innovative dance pieces, showcasing how AI can extend a choreographer's creative vocabulary.

6. AI in Culinary Arts

Project: Chef Watson by IBM

Details: IBM's Chef Watson used AI to analyze thousands of recipes and flavor profiles to suggest unique and innovative food combinations, assisting chefs in creating new dishes.

Outcome: Chef Watson demonstrated AI's potential in culinary creativity, offering chefs novel ingredient pairings and recipe ideas.

Conclusion

These examples reflect the diverse and multifaceted nature of human-AI collaborations in the creative sectors. They underscore AI's role not as a replacement for human creativity but as a powerful tool that can complement and enhance it, opening up new possibilities and pushing the boundaries of traditional artistic disciplines.

Strategies For Artists And Creators To Adapt And Thrive

As the landscape of art and creativity increasingly intersects with the world of Artificial Intelligence (AI), artists and creators must adapt to thrive in this new era. Here are some strategies that can help artists embrace AI and harness its potential to enhance their creative endeavors.

1. Embracing Lifelong Learning

Stay Informed About AI Trends: Artists should stay informed about the latest developments in AI technology and how they are being applied in their field.

Continuous Skill Development: Engaging in continuous learning, including online courses and workshops on AI and related digital tools, can keep artists updated and proficient in new technologies.

2. Experimentation with AI Tools

Hands-On Experience: Experimenting with different AI tools and platforms can help artists understand the capabilities and limitations of AI in their specific art form.

Creative Experimentation: Using AI for small-scale projects or experimental pieces can offer insights into how AI might fit into their broader creative practice.

3. Collaborative Partnerships

Engage with Technologists: Collaborating with AI developers, data scientists, and technologists can provide artists with valuable technical support and insights, leading to more successful integrations of AI in their work.

Cross-Disciplinary Projects: Participating in cross-disciplinary projects can expose artists to new ideas and methods, enriching their own creative process.

4. Ethical and Responsible Use of AI

Understanding Ethical Implications: Artists should be aware of the ethical implications of using AI, including issues related to data privacy, bias, and authorship.

Promoting Responsible Practices: Incorporating ethical considerations into their work with AI can position artists as responsible innovators in their field.

5. Adapting to Market Changes

Digital Marketing Skills: Developing digital marketing skills, such as social media marketing and online portfolio management, can help artists reach wider audiences and adapt to digital marketplaces.

Leveraging Online Platforms: Utilizing online platforms for showcasing and selling art, including AI-generated art, can open up new revenue streams.

6. Fostering Creativity and Originality

Blending AI with Traditional Techniques: Artists can combine AI with traditional artistic techniques, ensuring their work retains a unique human touch and stands out in the market.

Personalization of AI Tools: Customizing AI tools to fit their unique artistic style and vision can help artists maintain their individuality in their creations.

7. Networking and Community Engagement

Joining Art and Tech Communities: Participating in both art and tech communities can provide artists with networking opportunities, partnerships, and insights into how others are navigating the AI landscape.

Sharing Knowledge and Experiences: Contributing to forums, writing about their experiences, and speaking at events can help artists establish themselves as thought leaders in the intersection of art and AI.

Conclusion

Adapting to the AI era requires artists to be proactive, open-minded, and willing to step outside their comfort zones. By embracing lifelong learning, experimenting with AI tools, engaging in collaborative projects, and adapting to new market dynamics, artists and creators can not only survive but thrive, exploring new horizons of creativity and innovation.

Chapter 9: Harnessing AI For Enhanced Creativity

In Chapter 9, "Harnessing AI for Enhanced Creativity," we delve into the practicalities and potentials of utilizing Artificial Intelligence (AI) as a catalyst for creative innovation. This chapter is designed to guide artists, creators, and innovators in understanding and leveraging AI to augment and amplify their creative processes. Here, we explore the myriad ways in which AI can be a powerful ally in the realm of artistic creation, offering new perspectives, tools, and methodologies to expand the horizons of traditional and digital art forms.

As we navigate through this chapter, several key themes and areas of exploration will be covered:

Understanding AI's Creative Capabilities

Demystifying AI in Art: We begin with an overview of what AI in art entails, breaking down complex technical jargon into understandable concepts. This includes an exploration of how AI algorithms work and how they can be applied creatively.

AI's Role in Different Art Forms: We examine the specific roles and contributions of AI in various art forms, from visual arts and music to literature and performance arts, showcasing the versatility and adaptability of AI in creative contexts.

Practical Applications and Techniques

AI Tools and Software for Artists: This section introduces a range of AI tools, software, and platforms available to artists, along with guidance on how to use these tools effectively in different artistic mediums.

Techniques for Creative AI Collaboration: We explore techniques for successful collaboration between artists and AI, including how to guide AI systems in the creative process and how to interpret and refine AI-generated outputs.

Case Studies and Real-World Examples

Success Stories of AI in Creativity: The chapter features case studies and stories of artists and creators who have successfully integrated AI into their work, providing real-world examples and insights.

Lessons Learned and Best Practices: Drawing from these examples, we distill lessons learned and best practices for effectively harnessing AI in creative endeavors.

Navigating Challenges and Ethical Considerations

Overcoming Creative Challenges with AI: We address common challenges artists may face when working with AI, such as issues of control, unpredictability, and the integration of AI into existing creative workflows.

Ethical and Responsible AI Use: The chapter also delves into the ethical considerations in using AI for creativity, including discussions on intellectual property, artistic integrity, and responsible data usage.

Empowering Artists for the Future

Building AI Literacy in the Arts: We emphasize the importance of building AI literacy among artists and creators, equipping them with the knowledge and skills needed to navigate the AI-art landscape.

Vision for the Future: Finally, the chapter concludes with a forward-looking perspective, contemplating the evolving role of AI in the arts and its potential to redefine the boundaries of creativity and artistic expression.

In "Harnessing AI for Enhanced Creativity," we aim to provide a comprehensive, accessible, and inspiring guide for artists and creators to embrace AI, unlocking new creative potentials and navigating the exciting confluence of art and technology.

Practical Tips For Integrating AI Into Artistic Processes

Integrating Artificial Intelligence (AI) into artistic processes can be a transformative experience for creators. However, navigating this integration effectively requires understanding, strategy, and a bit of creativity. Here are some practical tips for artists looking to incorporate AI into their artistic workflows.

1. Start with Clear Objectives

Define Your Goals: Understand what you want to achieve with AI. Are you looking for new sources of inspiration, ways to automate certain tasks, or methods to explore new art forms?

Set Realistic Expectations: Recognize the capabilities and limitations of current AI technologies in relation to your artistic goals.

2. Familiarize Yourself with AI Tools

Explore and Experiment: Spend time exploring different AI tools and software that are relevant to your art form. This could include AI algorithms for image generation, music composition, text writing, etc.

Hands-On Practice: Experiment with these tools to understand their functionalities. Many AI tools offer trial versions or free tiers for beginners.

3. Educate Yourself

Learn the Basics: Gain a basic understanding of how AI works. Online courses, webinars, and workshops can be invaluable in building this foundational knowledge.

Stay Updated: AI technology evolves rapidly. Stay updated with the latest developments and how they might impact or benefit your artistic practice.

4. Collaborate and Network

Engage with the AI Art Community: Join forums, social media groups, or local communities focused on AI in art. Networking with other artists who use AI can provide insights and collaborative opportunities.

Seek Technical Expertise: If your project is complex, consider collaborating with technologists or AI experts who can bring in-depth technical skills to your artistic vision.

5. Integrate AI Gradually

Start Small: Begin by integrating AI into smaller aspects of your work before scaling up. This allows you to understand how AI can best complement your artistic style and process.

Iterative Process: Use an iterative approach, where you gradually refine how you use AI based on the outcomes and learning from each project.

6. Maintain Artistic Integrity

Keep Your Artistic Voice: Ensure that the use of AI doesn't overshadow your unique artistic voice. The goal is to use AI as a tool to enhance, not replace, your creative expression.

Ethical Considerations: Be mindful of ethical considerations, including the source of your AI's training data and the transparency in how you use AI in your creations.

7. Experiment with Different Applications

Diverse Applications: Don't limit AI to one aspect of your art. Experiment with various applications, from inspiration and concept development to execution and presentation.

Cross-Disciplinary Exploration: Explore how AI is used in other art forms for cross-disciplinary insights that could enrich your work.

8. Be Prepared for Challenges

Troubleshooting and Adaptation: Be prepared to troubleshoot technical issues and adapt your artistic process as needed when working with AI.

Balance Technology with Art: Strive for a balance where technology serves your art, rather than art serving the technology.

Conclusion

Integrating AI into artistic processes is a journey of exploration and learning. By starting with clear objectives, educating oneself, experimenting, and remaining open to new possibilities, artists can effectively harness the power of AI to push the boundaries of their creative expression.

Tools And Platforms Facilitating AI-Assisted Creativity

The landscape of AI-assisted creativity is rich with diverse tools and platforms, each offering unique capabilities to artists and creators. Here, we highlight some of these tools, categorizing them based on different artistic domains.

AI Tools for Visual Arts

DeepArt: Utilizes deep learning algorithms to transform photos into artworks in the style of famous painters like Van Gogh or Picasso.

RunwayML: A user-friendly platform that offers a variety of machine learning models for image and video creation, modification, and analysis.

GANpaint Studio: An interactive drawing tool that uses Generative Adversarial Networks (GANs) to create and alter images in a realistic manner.

AI Platforms for Music Composition

AIVA: An AI platform designed for composing symphonic music, using deep learning to generate music scores that can be used in films, games, and other mediums.

Amper Music: An AI music composition tool that enables users to create custom music tracks by specifying style, mood, and duration.

Jukedeck: Uses AI to create royalty-free music tracks tailored to specific genres, moods, and lengths (Note: As of my last update, Jukedeck was acquired by TikTok, so availability may vary).

AI-Driven Writing and Content Creation Tools

OpenAI's GPT-3: A state-of-the-art language processing AI capable of generating human-like text, useful for writing assistance, content generation, and more.

ShortlyAI: A writing tool based on GPT-3, designed to help with creative writing, including stories, poems, and other forms of content.

Sudowrite: Another tool built on GPT-3, aimed at assisting authors in overcoming writer's block and generating creative writing ideas and content.

AI for Film and Animation

RunwayML: Offers models specifically for video, allowing for tasks such as motion capture, green screen effects, and more.

EbSynth: A tool for transforming video footage into artistic animations using a single reference frame.

AI in Design and Architecture

DALL-E by OpenAI: An AI program capable of generating complex images from textual descriptions, useful for concept art and design inspiration.

ArchiGAN: A GAN-based tool that generates architectural models and urban design layouts from sketches.

AI for Interactive and Performance Arts

Google's Project Magenta: Provides tools and models for creating interactive and generative art, exploring the role of AI in the process of artistic creation.

TouchDesigner: A visual development platform that can integrate AI models for creating interactive media installations and performances.

Other Innovative Tools and Platforms

IBM Watson: Offers a range of AI services that can be applied in various creative contexts, from visual arts to music and writing.

Artbreeder: Uses GANs to allow users to create and modify images, particularly portraits, landscapes, and other artistic visuals.

Conclusion

These tools and platforms represent just a slice of the vast array of AI-assisted creative technologies available today. Each offers unique opportunities for artists and creators to explore new realms of creativity, pushing the boundaries of traditional artistic practices. Whether in visual arts, music, writing, or other domains, AI-assisted tools are becoming an integral part of the modern creative process.

Workshops, Courses, And Resources For Learning About AI

For artists, creatives, and enthusiasts looking to delve into the world of AI in the arts, there are numerous educational resources, workshops, and courses available. These platforms offer a range of learning opportunities, from beginner to advanced levels, catering to various interests and aspects of AI in creative fields.

Online Courses and Educational Platforms

Coursera: Offers courses like "AI For Everyone" by Andrew Ng and specialized courses in AI and machine learning. These can provide foundational knowledge useful for understanding AI applications in art.

Udemy: Features a variety of courses tailored to AI in creative sectors, including AI for music production, digital art, and more.

Kadenze: A platform specializing in art and creative technology, offering courses that often blend art with AI, coding, and digital media.

edX: Hosts courses from universities and institutions worldwide, including introductions to AI and more in-depth classes on specific AI technologies.

Workshops and Interactive Learning

AI Art Workshops: Various institutions and art collectives occasionally host workshops focused on AI art creation, offering hands-on experience with AI tools.

Meetups and Hackathons: Participating in local meetups or hackathons focused on AI and art can be a great way to learn in a collaborative environment.

Museum and Gallery Programs: Some contemporary art museums and galleries offer educational programs and workshops that explore the intersection of AI and art.

Online Communities and Forums

Art and AI Forums: Online forums and communities (like Reddit threads or specialized art and tech forums) can be valuable resources for advice, inspiration, and networking.

Social Media Groups: Platforms like Facebook and LinkedIn host groups dedicated to AI in art, where members share their work, experiences, and resources.

YouTube Channels: Numerous channels offer tutorials and insights on using AI in creative practices, ranging from beginner to advanced levels.

Books and Publications

"Artificial Intelligence and the Arts": This type of publication typically explores the theoretical and practical aspects of AI in various art forms.

Academic Journals: Journals like "Leonardo" on art, science, and technology often feature articles on AI's role in the creative sectors.

Specialized Blogs and Websites

Blogs by AI Artists and Experts: Following blogs and websites of artists who specialize in AI art can provide practical insights and updates on the latest trends and tools.

Technology and Art Websites: Websites that focus on the intersection of technology and art often publish articles, interviews, and tutorials related to AI in the arts.

University Programs and Courses

Formal Education Programs: Some universities now offer specialized courses or degrees at the intersection of AI and art, which can be an option for those seeking formal education in this field.

Conclusion

Whether you're a budding artist curious about AI or a seasoned creator looking to integrate AI into your work, the wealth of educational resources available offers a pathway for learning and exploration. From online courses and interactive workshops to community forums and academic studies, these resources provide the knowledge and skills necessary to navigate and innovate in the AI-infused landscape of contemporary art.

Chapter 10: The Renaissance Of Creativity – AI As A Tool

In Chapter 10, "The RenAIssance of Creativity – AI as a Tool, Not a Threat," we embark on a journey to redefine the narrative surrounding Artificial Intelligence (AI) in the creative realm. This chapter is an exploration into the harmonious coexistence of AI and human creativity, emphasizing AI's role as a powerful tool that enhances rather than diminishes the artistic process. We seek to dispel fears and misconceptions about AI, showcasing its potential to catalyze a new era of creative innovation – a true Renaissance of creativity in the digital age.

As we delve into this enlightening exploration, the chapter covers several crucial aspects:

Reframing the Perception of AI in Art

Debunking Myths: We address common myths about AI in the arts, such as the fear of human obsolescence, and provide a more balanced perspective on how AI can augment human creativity.

Celebrating Human-AI Collaboration: The focus is on successful collaborations between artists and AI, highlighting how these partnerships have led to groundbreaking work that neither could achieve alone.

AI as a Creative Amplifier

Expanding Creative Boundaries: We explore how AI can push the boundaries of traditional art forms, introducing new genres and techniques that were previously unimaginable.

AI in Creative Problem Solving: The chapter discusses how AI can assist in the creative process, from providing inspiration to solving complex design and compositional challenges.

Educational and Professional Development

AI Literacy in Art Education: We emphasize the importance of incorporating AI literacy in art education, preparing the next generation of artists for a future where AI is an integral part of the creative process.

Career Opportunities: The chapter also explores new career paths and opportunities emerging at the intersection of AI and art, encouraging artists to embrace AI as a means of enhancing their professional repertoire.

Ethical and Responsible Use of AI

Navigating Ethical Considerations: We delve into the ethical implications of using AI in art, including issues of authorship, intellectual property, and the responsible use of AI-generated content.

Promoting Sustainable Practices: The chapter advocates for sustainable and ethical practices in the use of AI in art, ensuring that the integration of technology aligns with broader societal and environmental values.

AI as a Gateway to Global Artistic Exchange

Fostering Global Connections: We discuss how AI can serve as a bridge, connecting artists across the globe and facilitating cross-cultural collaborations and exchanges.

AI in Preserving Cultural Heritage: The role of AI in preserving and reinterpreting cultural heritage and traditional art forms is also highlighted, showcasing its potential in keeping diverse cultural expressions alive in the digital era.

Conclusion

"The RenAIssance of Creativity – AI as a Tool, Not a Threat" aims to inspire a paradigm shift in how we view AI in the arts. By focusing on AI's role as a collaborative tool, this chapter encourages artists, creators, and enthusiasts to embrace AI, unlocking new dimensions of creativity and charting a course towards a future where technology and human ingenuity synergistically co-create the art of tomorrow.

Redefining The Role Of The Artist In The Age Of AI

In the age of Artificial Intelligence (AI), the role of the artist is undergoing a significant transformation. This shift challenges traditional notions of creativity, authorship, and the artistic process, inviting a redefinition of what it means to be an artist. Here, we explore how the emergence of AI in the creative world is reshaping the artist's role.

Collaboration with Technology

The Artist as a Director: In the AI era, artists increasingly assume the role of directors or orchestrators, guiding the AI in the creative process, setting parameters, and refining outputs to align with their artistic vision.

Interdisciplinary Skill Sets: Artists are now required to develop interdisciplinary skill sets, combining artistic sensibility with a basic understanding of AI and data. This combination allows for more effective utilization of AI as a creative tool.

Evolving Creative Processes

Enhanced Creativity: AI opens new avenues for creativity, allowing artists to explore complex ideas and visualizations that may be challenging to achieve manually. This expansion can lead to novel and innovative artworks.

Iterative Experimentation: The creative process becomes more iterative with AI, involving a cycle of input, generation, refinement, and redevelopment, allowing artists to explore a broader range of creative possibilities.

New Forms of Expression

Hybrid Art Forms: The convergence of AI and traditional art forms is giving rise to hybrid genres, where digital and physical mediums merge, creating new avenues for artistic expression.

Interactive and Generative Art: AI enables the creation of interactive and generative art, where artworks are dynamic and responsive, offering unique experiences to each viewer.

Ethical and Philosophical Considerations

Navigating Authorship and Originality: Artists working with AI face new ethical and philosophical questions regarding authorship and originality. They must navigate the nuances of creating with a tool that has its own 'creative' capabilities.

Addressing Bias and Cultural Sensitivity: Artists must be aware of and address biases inherent in AI algorithms, ensuring their art does not inadvertently perpetuate stereotypes or cultural insensitivities.

Adaptation and Continuous Learning

Lifelong Learning: The rapid evolution of AI technologies necessitates a commitment to lifelong learning and adaptability for artists. Staying abreast of technological advances and continuously evolving their practice is crucial.

Collaborative Networks: Building networks with technologists, other artists, and AI communities becomes essential, facilitating knowledge exchange and collaboration in an increasingly interdisciplinary art world.

Conclusion

The role of the artist in the age of AI is not diminishing but rather evolving in exciting and complex ways. This era provides artists with unprecedented tools and opportunities to push the boundaries of their creativity. By embracing AI, artists can redefine their practices, create innovative works, and contribute to the ongoing discourse on the future of art in the digital age.

Encouraging A Culture Of Experimentation

In the rapidly evolving landscape where art intersects with Artificial Intelligence (AI), fostering a culture of experimentation and innovation is crucial. This culture not only embraces the transformative potential of AI in the arts but also encourages artists, creators, and institutions to explore new frontiers of creativity. Here's how such a culture can be nurtured and sustained.

Embracing Risk and Experimentation

Encourage Trial and Error: Cultivate an environment where trial and error are embraced, and failure is viewed as a stepping stone to innovation. This approach encourages artists to experiment with AI without the fear of immediate perfection.

Promote Interdisciplinary Collaboration: Foster collaborations that bring together artists, technologists, scientists, and thinkers from diverse fields. Such intersections often lead to breakthrough ideas and innovative applications of AI in art.

Providing Resources and Platforms

Access to AI Tools and Training: Ensure artists have access to AI tools and necessary training. This could be through workshops, online resources, or collaborative projects with tech companies and AI labs.

Creating Platforms for Showcase: Develop platforms where experimental works involving AI can be showcased. This includes exhibitions, online galleries, and festivals dedicated to digital and AI-assisted art.

Nurturing a Supportive Community

Building Networks and Communities: Encourage the formation of networks and communities where artists can share experiences, learn from each other, and find support for their experimental projects.

Mentorship Programs: Establish mentorship programs where experienced artists and technologists guide newcomers in navigating the complexities of integrating AI into their creative processes.

Educational Initiatives

Integrate AI into Art Education: Update art education curricula to include AI, teaching not just the technical aspects but also how it can be applied creatively.

Host Lectures and Seminars: Organize talks, lectures, and seminars focusing on the intersection of AI and art, highlighting innovative projects and discussing future trends.

Encouraging Ethical and Sustainable Practices

Ethical Experimentation: Embed discussions on ethics within the experimentation process, encouraging artists to consider the implications of their AI-assisted artworks.

Sustainability in AI Art: Promote practices that consider the environmental impact of AI technologies, advocating for sustainable approaches in digital art creation.

Funding and Grants

Financial Support for Experimental Projects: Provide grants, scholarships, and funding opportunities specifically for projects that explore new uses of AI in art.

Sponsorship and Partnerships: Encourage sponsorships and partnerships between art institutions and tech companies to fund and support experimental and innovative projects.

Conclusion

By encouraging a culture of experimentation and innovation, the art world can fully harness the potential of AI as a transformative tool. This culture not only propels artistic creativity to new heights but also ensures a dynamic and inclusive future for the intersection of art and technology.

Case Studies Of Groundbreaking Works Created With AI

The integration of Artificial Intelligence (AI) in the creative process has led to the creation of several groundbreaking works across various art forms. These case studies exemplify how AI assistance can lead to innovative and thought-provoking art, pushing the boundaries of traditional creativity.

1. AI in Visual Arts: "Memories of Passersby I" by Mario Klingemann

Background: Mario Klingemann, a pioneer in the use of AI and neural networks for artistic creation, created "Memories of Passersby I", a generative art installation.

AI Technology Used: Klingemann used a series of neural networks to generate an endless stream of portraits, displayed on vintage monitors.

Significance: The work is a milestone in generative art, showcasing how AI can create art that is ever-changing and unique, and it also raises questions about the role of the artist and the creative process.

2. AI in Music: "Hello World" Album by SKYGGE

Background: "Hello World" is the first full-length music album co-composed with AI, spearheaded by French musician Benoit Carré, also known as SKYGGE.

AI Technology Used: The album was created using the Flow Machines software, which analyzes a vast database of songs to create music in various styles.

Significance: This project demonstrated the potential of AI in expanding the capabilities of musicians and redefining the process of music composition.

3. AI in Literature: "1 the Road" by Ross Goodwin

Background: Artist and technologist Ross Goodwin embarked on a road trip with an AI in a laptop hooked up to various sensors, intending to write a novel.

AI Technology Used: The AI used inputs from the sensors, including location, time, nearby sounds, and images, to write prose in real-time.

Significance: "1 the Road" challenges traditional notions of authorship and highlights AI's potential in literary creativity.

4. AI in Film: "Zone Out" by Richard Ramchurn

Background: Richard Ramchurn's "Zone Out" is an AI-assisted film where the narrative changes based on the viewer's brain activity.

AI Technology Used: The film uses an electroencephalogram (EEG) headset to measure the viewer's attention, and AI algorithms change the scenes accordingly.

Significance: This film explores interactive storytelling and the potential of AI to create personalized viewing experiences.

5. AI in Dance and Performance: "Levitation" by Huang Yi

Background: "Levitation" is a dance performance featuring Taiwanese dancer and choreographer Huang Yi and a robot programmed with AI.

AI Technology Used: The robot, equipped with AI, interacts and dances with Huang, creating a seamless performance between human and machine.

Significance: This performance exemplifies the potential of AI in enhancing performing arts and exploring new forms of artistic expression.

Conclusion

These case studies demonstrate the diverse and innovative ways in which AI can assist in the creative process, producing works that redefine the boundaries of art. They highlight not only the potential of AI as a tool in various art forms but also raise important questions about creativity, collaboration, and the future of art in the AI era.

Chapter 11: The Future Symbiosis Of Human And AI

In Chapter 11, "The Future Symbiosis of Human and Artificial Creativity," we embark on an exploratory journey into the not-so-distant future where human ingenuity and artificial intelligence (AI) converge in a seamless and symbiotic relationship. This chapter is dedicated to unraveling the potentialities, challenges, and transformative impacts of this alliance on the creative landscape. As AI technologies continue to evolve and permeate the arts, a new era of collaborative creativity is emerging, reshaping our understanding of the creative process and the nature of art itself.

As we navigate this chapter, several key themes are explored:

Exploring the Convergence of Human and AI Creativity

Synergistic Collaboration: We examine how the collaboration between human creativity and AI is evolving, moving beyond AI as merely a tool, to AI as a creative partner capable of contributing actively to the artistic process.

Redefining Artistic Creation: This section delves into how this symbiosis is redefining what it means to create art, blending human emotional depth with AI's vast data-processing capabilities and algorithmic precision.

The Evolution of Creative Processes

Transformative Workflows: We explore how traditional creative workflows are being transformed by AI integration, leading to new methods of ideation, design, and execution across various artistic disciplines.

AI-Driven Innovation in Art Forms: This part of the chapter highlights innovative examples across visual arts, music, literature, and performance, where the fusion of AI and human creativity is producing groundbreaking work.

Ethical and Philosophical Implications

Navigating the Ethical Terrain: We address the ethical implications of this symbiosis, including questions of authorship, authenticity, and the ethical use of AI in creating art.

Philosophical Considerations: The chapter also contemplates the philosophical aspects of this partnership, pondering the nature of creativity and the role of human intuition in an AI-augmented creative process.

Preparing for a Collaborative Future

Educational Shifts: We discuss the necessary shifts in art education and training to prepare upcoming artists for this collaborative future, emphasizing the need for interdisciplinary learning that bridges art and technology.

Adapting to Market Changes: The chapter also covers how the art market and industries related to creative fields are adapting to the integration of AI, including new platforms for distribution, exhibition, and monetization.

Envisioning the Future

Predictions and Possibilities: We present predictions and scenarios for the future of this symbiosis, imagining the potential developments and innovations that could arise from this confluence of human and artificial creativity.

Challenges and Opportunities: Finally, the chapter acknowledges the challenges of this evolving landscape while highlighting the immense opportunities for creative exploration and expression it presents.

In "The Future Symbiosis of Human and Artificial Creativity," the chapter invites readers to envisage a future where AI is not seen as a replacement for human creativity but as a complement to it, opening up new realms of artistic possibility and redefining the essence of creative expression in the digital age.

Vision For A Future

In envisioning a future where Artificial Intelligence (AI) and human creativity coexist harmoniously, we imagine a world where the boundaries between technology and art are seamlessly blended. This future landscape is one where AI serves as a catalyst and enhancer of human creative expression, rather than a substitute or adversary. Let's explore the contours of this envisioned future.

Collaborative Creation

Synergy in Artistic Processes: Artists and AI collaborate, with AI offering new tools and perspectives that complement human intuition and creativity. This partnership leads to novel forms of art that neither could achieve independently.

Interactive Art: Art becomes more interactive and responsive, with AI enabling artworks that adapt to and engage with audiences in real-time, providing personalized experiences.

Expanded Creative Boundaries

Uncharted Artistic Territories: AI helps artists explore uncharted territories in creativity. From generating new forms of visual art to composing complex musical pieces, AI acts as a bridge to realms of imagination that were previously inaccessible.

Diverse Artistic Expressions: AI's ability to process and learn from a vast array of cultural styles and historical data leads to more diverse and inclusive artistic expressions.

Enhanced Learning and Accessibility

AI in Art Education: AI becomes an integral part of art education, providing tools for learning and exploration, and offering students the ability to experiment with advanced technologies.

Democratization of Art: The barrier to entry for creating art lowers significantly, as AI tools enable more people to engage in creative activities, regardless of their traditional artistic skills.

Ethical and Sustainable Development

Responsible AI Use: The art world adopts ethical guidelines for AI use, ensuring that AI-driven art respects privacy, cultural diversity, and artistic integrity.

Sustainable Practices: AI technologies are developed and utilized in sustainable ways, mindful of environmental impacts and promoting longevity and preservation in art.

Cultural and Economic Shifts

Global Artistic Collaboration: AI facilitates global collaboration, breaking down geographical and cultural barriers, leading to a rich exchange of ideas and artistic fusion.

New Economic Models: The art market adapts to include AI-generated art, with new platforms and economic models emerging for the distribution and monetization of AI-driven artworks.

Redefining the Role of Artists

Artists as Visionaries and Innovators: The role of the artist evolves, with artists becoming visionaries who harness AI to realize their creative visions and drive innovation in art.

Continuous Adaptation and Learning: Artists continually adapt and expand their skills, embracing lifelong learning to stay abreast of technological advancements in AI.

Conclusion

The harmonious coexistence of AI and human creativity ushers in a new era – a RenAIssance – characterized by unparalleled creativity and innovation. In this future, AI is not a threat to human creativity but a valuable ally that enriches and diversifies the artistic landscape. This vision for the future is not only inspiring but also attainable, promising a world where art transcends traditional boundaries and becomes a more inclusive and dynamic force in society.

Ethical Guidelines For AI In The Arts

As Artificial Intelligence (AI) becomes increasingly integrated into the arts, establishing ethical guidelines and best practices is essential to ensure responsible and beneficial use. These guidelines can help artists, technologists, and institutions navigate the complexities of AI in creative processes while respecting both artistic integrity and societal norms.

1. Transparency and Disclosure

Openness About AI Involvement: Clearly disclose the use of AI in the creation of an artwork. Audiences should be informed about the role AI played in the creative process.

Honesty in Representation: Represent AI-assisted works accurately in exhibitions, galleries, and sales platforms, avoiding misleading claims about the nature of the artwork.

2. Intellectual Property and Authorship

Clear Attribution: Establish clear guidelines for attribution and authorship when AI is used. This includes crediting AI programmers, designers, as well as the AI system itself, if applicable.

Respecting Intellectual Property: Ensure that the use of AI does not infringe on the intellectual property rights of others, including respect for the datasets used for training AI models.

3. Ethical Use of Data

Consent and Privacy: Use data ethically and responsibly, ensuring that any data used to train AI systems, especially personal data, is gathered with consent and protected appropriately.

Bias and Fairness: Be aware of and actively work to mitigate biases in AI algorithms that may reflect or perpetuate societal, racial, or gender biases.

4. Cultural Sensitivity and Diversity

Promote Diversity: Use AI as a tool to promote diversity in art, ensuring that it supports a wide range of cultural expressions and perspectives.

Cultural Respect: Be mindful of cultural sensitivities and avoid using AI to appropriate or misrepresent cultural artifacts and practices.

5. Sustainable and Responsible AI Use

Environmental Considerations: Be conscious of the environmental impact of using AI, including the energy consumption of training and running AI models.

Long-term Preservation: Consider the long-term preservation and compatibility of AI-generated artworks, ensuring that they can be maintained, archived, and accessed in the future.

6. Continuous Learning and Adaptation

Stay Informed: Keep abreast of the latest developments and discussions in AI ethics, especially as they pertain to the arts.

Adaptive Practices: Continuously adapt and update ethical guidelines and best practices to reflect new developments and understandings in the field of AI.

7. Collaborative and Inclusive Development

Inclusive Development: Involve a diverse range of voices, including artists, technologists, ethicists, and representatives from various cultural backgrounds, in developing and refining AI tools for the arts.

Public Engagement: Engage with the public and artistic communities on the ethical use of AI in art, fostering a broader understanding and dialogue.

Conclusion

The establishment of ethical guidelines and best practices for AI in the arts is a collaborative and ongoing process. It requires a balance between embracing the innovative potential of AI and acknowledging the responsibilities that come with integrating new technologies into the creative world. By adhering to these guidelines, the artistic community can lead the way in responsible and ethical AI use, ensuring that AI enhances rather than detracts from the rich tapestry of human creativity.

Final Thoughts...

As we reach the conclusion of our exploration into the intricate and evolving relationship between Artificial Intelligence (AI) and creativity, it's clear that we stand at the threshold of a new era in artistic expression. The integration of AI into the arts is not just a technological phenomenon but a cultural and creative revolution that is redefining the boundaries of what can be imagined and created.

Embracing a New Creative Paradigm

AI as an Extension of Human Creativity: AI should be seen as an extension of human creativity, a tool that opens up new possibilities rather than a replacement for human ingenuity. It offers artists a new palette of options to express their vision and ideas.

The Potential for Unprecedented Art Forms: With AI, we are witnessing the emergence of art forms and expressions that were previously inconceivable. AI's ability to process vast amounts of data and learn from it can lead to unique artistic outputs, enriching the diversity of human creativity.

Balancing Innovation with Ethical Considerations

Ethical Use of AI in Art: As AI becomes more ingrained in the creative process, ethical considerations become increasingly important. Issues of data privacy, bias, and cultural sensitivity must be at the forefront of discussions about AI in art.

Maintaining Artistic Integrity: While embracing AI's capabilities, it's crucial to maintain artistic integrity and ensure that the use of AI aligns with the artist's vision and ethical standards.

The Future of Artistic Collaboration

Collaboration Between Artists and AI: The future of art will likely see deeper collaborations between artists and AI, where AI's role evolves from a tool to a creative partner, capable of contributing actively to the creative process.

Cross-Disciplinary Partnerships: The intersection of AI and art encourages cross-disciplinary partnerships, bringing together artists, technologists, scientists, and thinkers, fostering a rich environment for innovation and creativity.

Education and Accessibility

Adapting Art Education: Art education needs to adapt to this changing landscape, integrating AI literacy and providing training in how to effectively use AI in the creative process.

Democratizing Art Creation: AI has the potential to democratize art creation, making it more accessible to people with varying skills and backgrounds, thus widening the scope of who can participate in the creation of art.

Looking Forward

A Continuously Evolving Landscape: The relationship between AI and creativity is continuously evolving, with new advancements in AI technology opening up further possibilities.

An Optimistic Outlook: While there are challenges to navigate, the future of AI in the arts is optimistic. It promises a world where technology and human creativity coalesce to create art that is more diverse, inclusive, and expressive than ever before.

Conclusion

In conclusion, the journey of AI and creativity is one of collaboration and innovation, a fusion of the computational with the emotional and intuitive. As we move forward, this partnership promises to not only transform how we create and experience art but also deepen our understanding of the very nature of creativity. The future of AI in the arts is a canvas of limitless potential, awaiting the bold strokes of artists and innovators worldwide.

Ideas for Using AI for Creativity:

Collaborative Art Creation: Pairing artists with AI to produce unique artworks that blend human emotion and AI's computational power.

AI as a Tool for Education: Using AI to teach art techniques, history, and theory, adapting to each student's learning style.

Music Composition and Experimentation: AI algorithms that help musicians create new sounds and compositions.

Writing and Storytelling Assistance: AI tools that suggest plot ideas, character developments, or even write sections of text.

Digital Art Filters and Effects: Using AI to transform photographs and videos into different art styles.

Performance Arts and Choreography: AI systems that help choreograph dance performances or theatrical productions.

Interactive Art Installations: Creating art installations that use AI to interact with audiences in real-time.

Enhancing Art Accessibility: AI that helps translate art into formats accessible to people with disabilities.

Art Market Analysis: AI tools that analyze trends and provide insights for artists and galleries.

Preservation and Restoration: Using AI to predict deterioration and suggest restoration techniques for historical artworks.